What people are saying about …

Throw the First Punch

"The way Beth tells stories and addresses spiritual warfare in a fun and approachable manner makes *Throw the First Punch* a meaningful read. She helps us see kingdom truths for their upside-downness—we are more powerful than we know and more loved than we can imagine. The idea of punching our enemy first? Game changer."

Bob Goff, *New York Times* bestselling author of
Love Does, Everybody Always, and *Dream Big*

"Like an Olympic-wrestler-turned-coach, Beth Guckenberger offers us not only a compelling vision but also hands-on guidance in the critical practices and posture, grips and maneuvers of a vibrant spiritual life. I've seen firsthand: Beth lives what she teaches. This is no abstract treatise. It is a field guide for a life of holy combat."

Jedd Medefind, president of Christian
Alliance for Orphans

"For the believer in Jesus who wants wisdom for standing strong (and long) in the battle, this is for you. Beth comes alongside the reader in truthful love to equip you to endure and go on the offensive. Through its engaging stories, deep exploration of Scripture, and practical applications, this book will equip you to throw the first punch!"

Michayla White, executive director of INCM

"Think of *Throw the First Punch* as a tactical manual for warriors of faith who want to take more ground for Jesus Christ, push back darkness, and be very effective instruments for the destruction of evil. Lock in on the truth Beth shares, and the Enemy will certainly be on alarm every day because of the damage you will do to his schemes."

Steve Biondo, president of the Tim Tebow Foundation

"I have always appreciated Beth's spiritually aggressive posture. Her personal history of making bold, loving moves is an inspiring model for us all to follow. *Throw the First Punch* is raw and real, sharing Beth's cautionary tales and personal victories. We need more practical battle plans like this. Highly recommend!"

Brian Tome, founding and senior pastor of Crossroads Church

"I absolutely love Beth's passion for Jesus, for the gospel, and for people. This book is a great weapon in our spiritual arsenal to help us live and love like Jesus. Beth teaches us how to battle the Enemy in a biblical way that is wise, honest, and fully practical."

Matt Massey, lead pastor of Vineyard Community Church

"Beth reminds us that we must live present lives and always be spiritually aware. The old saying 'the best offense is a great defense' truly seems accurate, as Beth helps the reader understand the posture and position Christ followers need to take to successfully combat the lies of the Enemy."

Greg Lucid, president of Lucid Artist

"Your soul needs this book. You will be drawn closer to Jesus. You will be empowered and equipped to live boldly and victoriously. Beth vividly illustrates Christ within us is more powerful than the evil around us. One of the best books I've ever read."

Andy Lehman, vice president of Lifesong for Orphans

"*Throw the First Punch* makes it clear that God has empowered and equipped us to declare war on and defeat the Enemy. As an anointed storyteller, Beth Guckenberger brings biblical truth to life as one who has experienced the victory that only comes from following and living for Jesus. Transparent and powerful—it's the call for all of us to suit up!"

Tami Heim, president and CEO of
Christian Leadership Alliance

"The rules of warfare are to know your enemy and to gather all intelligence on his nature. Beth has done both. This is not a 'demon behind every bush' book. It is truth, reality, and warnings of the Enemy of our soul: Satan. With sound biblical teaching and real life stories, this book equips us with weapons of spiritual warfare that embolden us to walk wisely and boldly in faith. We need this insight and practical instruction."

Jerry White, PhD, international president emeritus of
The Navigators, Major General, US Air Force (ret.)

"Many Christian and self-help books address common causes of struggles, including causes that are emotional or psychological, physical or medical, social or political. Beth has unveiled an added spiritual dimension that is often neglected, by writing with candor and vulnerability about the ageless struggle between good and evil. She provides refreshing insights into how 'working within God's power, we can learn to use God's [spiritual] tools' as effective help along the way—including praise, prayer, and Scripture."

Susan Hillis, PhD, speaker, writer,
scientist, adoptive mother of 11

"*Throw the First Punch* provides a critical reminder that there will always be another battle in life and that we need to be ready and equipped for the fight.

Beth provides great insight and practical advice on how to lace up your gloves and let God's light and power land the punch that assures the victory."

Edward Martin, Chief Omniwin
Officer of 5thelement.group

"In a season when the conditions of this world press on our exhaustion button, we wonder, is it time to just give up? This book will ground you, refresh you, and empower you. Beth cleverly exposes the schemes of the Enemy and equips readers with the hope that they are more than conquerors in Jesus. I encourage everyone to let this book be a powerful reminder of how to thrive again, find peace again, and hope again."

Lori Bethran, senior director of children's
ministries at Lakewood Church, Houston, TX

THROW THE
FIRST PUNCH

THROW THE FIRST PUNCH

DEFEATING THE ENEMY HELL-BENT ON YOUR DESTRUCTION

BETH GUCKENBERGER

DAVID C COOK

transforming lives together

THROW THE FIRST PUNCH
Published by David C Cook
4050 Lee Vance Drive
Colorado Springs, CO 80918 U.S.A.

Integrity Music Limited, a Division of David C Cook
Brighton, East Sussex BN1 2RE, England

The graphic circle C logo is a registered trademark of David C Cook.

Bible credits are listed in the back of the book.

Library of Congress Control Number 2021944182
ISBN 978-0-8307-8257-4
eISBN 978-0-8307-8258-1

The Team: Michael Covington, Stephanie Bennett,
James Hershberger, Jack Campbell, Susan Murdock
Cover Design: Nick Lee
Author cover photo: Brian Steege (rep. Etc Creative, Inc.)

Printed in the United States of America
First Edition 2022

1 2 3 4 5 6 7 8 9 10

092021

To Todd: You are the best kingdom warrior I know.

"He trains my hands for war."
Psalm 144:1

About the Author

Beth Guckenberger is a sought-after speaker and lifelong missionary who communicates on stage, radio, film, and in print how God works in her life. She and her husband, Todd, lead Back2Back Ministries, an international orphan-care organization where staff work relentlessly to find creative solutions to the challenges facing vulnerable children and their families. They lived in Monterrey, Mexico, for fifteen years and now reside in Cincinnati, Ohio, where Back2Back Ministries has its US office.

Beth and Todd are the parents of eleven children, a family they've formed of biological, foster, and adoptive children. Beth has written ten books and speaks extensively about her experiences as a mother, nonprofit leader, and student of God's Word.

Beth's best days end with meaningful conversation, fresh air, and a good meal. Lately her favorite quote is "Be the kind of woman that when your feet hit the floor each morning, the Devil says, 'Oh crap! She's up!'"

Contents

Part III: Standing Strong

Don't lose momentum. Pick up the 21-day guided journal **Punch First** so you can take the next step once you're finished reading this book.

(Find a sample of the journal in the "What's Next?" section in the back of this book.)

Preface

A few years ago, I agreed to speak for two consecutive weekends at a church on the topic of spiritual warfare. At the time, a friend of mine was going through a difficult situation and I was seeing firsthand how the Enemy circles around the wounded. Prior to my visit, the leadership called to tell me that one of the services was on "Family Sunday" and children would be included in the service. "You can still cover the same topic—just keep it PG," they requested.

I decided to share openly with these young families in an attempt to de-caricaturize Satan. We talked about how the Enemy loves the dark and the way he stokes our feelings of fear or anxiety at night. He doesn't drip in blood and carry a pitchfork. He doesn't just live on porn sites and in faraway countries. We talked about conflict and how Satan is a third party present in every struggle. He actively tries to destroy me and all that's true. I needed to learn to look for him and call him out when he was using me to further his agenda. I told them I was tired of the teaching that said to put on your spiritual armor and get ready for when he comes at you. Instead, I wanted to play offense and not defense. I asked, why can't we learn to punch him first?

I wasn't sure how my message would be received. The biggest shock coming out of those weeks was the congregation's response. Men and women came up to me and sent me messages asking how they could protect their families and themselves. They brought up powerful questions about how to be aware of the Devil and effectively fight against him. People were hungry for straight talk about spiritual warfare and its implications for our marriages, families, children, and friendships.

Problems come at us every day in the form of broken relationships, disappointments at work, challenges with physical health, and spiritual attacks. Heaviness and grief can settle over small things as well as large losses. It can be tempting to think it will all be better when our circumstances change. But the Bible tells us *there will always be another battle.* In 2 Samuel 21, David and his men were constantly confronted with yet "another battle," and so too will we. Instead of fearing or attempting to avoid the battle, though, we need to be prepared for it and face it head-on.

Initially, it intimidated me to write down my stories and thoughts on this subject; I thought for sure it would be like waving a red flag in front of a bull. However, I once interviewed author Anne Lamott, and when I asked her what writing advice she had for me, she said to write something "you would be delighted to stumble upon." I couldn't shake the sense that I would be delighted for someone to vulnerably share how sometimes the Enemy had won in their lives, but other times he had taken a black eye. What was the difference? What was the fallout? Could someone stop pretending and just be plainspoken about a topic we typically either exaggerate or avoid?

I began asking a single question before every date night with my husband, every meeting at work, every parenting challenge, and every difficult friendship conversation. The answers to this question enabled me to draw up a spiritual-combat plan in each situation. The question: *If I were the Enemy, what would I want to happen here?*

I saw patterns in the answers, and the reassuring thing is that these patterns are old stories. This is a battle we've already won! He isn't all that creative or clever; he's been doing the same things over and over again. We can anticipate his moves and make choices to block his success. We don't need to cower or shudder. God is undefeated. He has never lost, He never will, and He wants us on His team!

When I know the Enemy's plan, what's the next step? What does that look like? When I feel any number of hard or big feelings, how can I practically activate spiritual strength and not just hold ground, but take some of it back? Those unfiltered experiences and conversations with family and friends—and the answers we processed together—are in the coming chapters. Let's learn to throw the first punch!

Acknowledgments

To my front-porch friends whom I have walked alongside and they with me: this is sharing the work and study we've done with others. I am so thankful for the conversations of substance we've had and the fighting we've done for each other.

I am part of a large Back2Back family, and I am grateful for the ministry team I labor alongside. Wherever in the world you are working with orphaned and vulnerable children and their families, I love and appreciate you. #iiiyi To Jenna, we are a great example of 1+1 equaling more than 2. So grateful to share stories, lists, and fruit with you.

To Bryan, I say this every time: I would do this whole thing just to work with you! Thank you for cheering me on and having a seat for me at the Alive table.

To the Cook team: I told you creatives work best when we feel safe, and you make it easy to feel free and supported!

To my mom, I've said it on a thousand stages: I learned how to love Jesus from watching you. Thank you for cheering me on and listening to my endless stories.

To my kids, I know there are costs and benefits to having a mom who tells stories. Thank you for counting the costs and sharing with me in the benefits. I am grateful you walk together in this journey of trusting God. Let's keep fighting against an enemy and standing up for each other. You have taught me over and over again that love makes a family. I am crazy proud of each of you.

To Todd, I don't have the words. There is no one who has fought more for or alongside me. Even under the fiercest attack, I love looking over and seeing you.

Introduction

While I was serving as a missionary in Mexico, our ministry campus was hosting a large youth group for spring break. One night, the worship and sharing were going late with students spontaneously confessing their sin and singing. The younger youth pastor asked if I would stay up with him so we could respond to the students together. God was doing something we didn't see every night, and neither of us wanted it to stop. I took a break from being up front and stood with one of our interns in the back of the large, outdoor, thatched-roof structure. We swayed to the music, both caught up in it all, feeling joyful and peaceful.

I closed my eyes, and when I opened them a moment later, I caught a glimpse of a young high school couple slipping out the back, hand in hand. They were walking toward a gate that connected to a new piece of property we were renovating and, therefore, was considered dangerous and off-limits. In the middle of the property sat the eyesore of an abandoned warehouse we would eventually tear down, but for the time being it was keeping building materials out of the elements. (Neighbors told us terrible stories of how in the past, the police had used it for off-site and off-the-books interrogations. I never knew exactly what to believe, but when we later excavated the land, we found plenty of evidence of prior shady activity.)

Ever since we purchased the land, we encountered unexplainable setbacks and frequently heard strange sounds coming from that area. My husband,

Todd, said the noises reminded him of the shrieking monkeys from *The Wizard of Oz*. Machinery broke down, permits were delayed, and workers got hurt. You could almost stand with one leg on our current campus and one leg over there, bobbing back and forth, and feel the difference between darkness and light. We joked about it in the beginning, then it stopped being funny. We were building foster homes for families to care for orphaned and vulnerable teenagers, and we knew one day the land would be full of light. But to be honest, at this point, it just felt dark, like it had some leftover shadows we still needed to dispel.

I said to Kim, the intern standing beside me, "I don't even like going over there in the daytime, let alone at night, but we need to shoo them back over here. My guess is the two lovebirds are looking for a moment of privacy. Will you come with me?" She hesitated long enough that I knew she was thinking about the boogeyman as much as I was, but she eventually nodded, then we slipped out the back and through the makeshift gate. I grew up pretty theologically conservative, so while I had experienced spiritual gifts and spiritual warfare, it was still fuzzy to me exactly what Satan could do and where he could do it. As we headed out into the dark, I hoped my memorized verse "Greater is he that is in you than he that is in the world" (1 John 4:4 ASV) would be enough to protect me.

There was no power on that side of the property, and it took a minute for our eyes to adjust. I walked toward the *bodega*, the abandoned warehouse, which had an opening on each side large enough to drive a truck through. I stood on one end and scanned the dark corners, using the moonlight to look for the couple's outlines. I could see lumber stacked to one side and cement bags lining the walls. The building was more than two stories tall and, even though well swept, seemed dirty inside to me.

Then I saw *something*. I didn't know what I was looking at; it definitely wasn't the teens we were on the hunt for. It was tall—much taller than me—maybe nine feet high. It was lit, as if glowing, and my first thought was it looked like an angel. It had wings and was getting brighter the longer I looked at it. My hand flew to my mouth, and without thinking, I said loudly, "Oh. My. *Jesus!*" I wasn't taking the Lord's name in vain; I was simply calling out for Him, or to Him. As soon as I said "Jesus," "it" got down on all fours and scrambled out of sight, moving as I imagined a gargoyle might. A shiver ran up my spine and I knew whatever it was, it wasn't good.

I immediately turned and ran as fast as I could, forgetting about the couple, the intern, and the worshipping teenagers. When I got to my house, I slammed shut the heavy metal front door behind me as I took the stairs two at a time. Bursting into our bedroom, I lunged for the bed where Todd was already asleep. I practically screamed at him to wake up: "I just saw a demon. Holy crap. It looked like light. Oh my gosh. Oh my Jesus." I was shaking, babbling, crying, and simultaneously picking up the phone to call my mother in Ohio as if she were 911.

Todd, now completely awake, sprang to his feet, ready for action. "Who are you calling? Where is it?" Of the fight, flight, or freeze options, he's definitely a fighter.

"I'm calling my mom. I have to ask her. She'll know. She'll know if it's real. She's read her Bible front to back and back to front …" I wasn't even making sense as I rambled to Todd.

It was after midnight, but she answered on the first ring. You do that when the phone rings at that hour. *"Mom!"* I started in on her without a greeting. "Mom, can we see angels? Can people see angels? Or more like demons? Can *people* see into the spiritual realm?!" I burst into fresh tears.

She quietly asked me questions about what I had seen and, after listening to me recount the whole story, said, "Yes, if that's what you saw, then I would say yes. God gave you the ability in that moment to see what we know has always been there." She would later send me Job 4:15, "A spirit glided past my face, and the hair on my body stood on end."

The next day, I couldn't talk about it. I managed only to check in and confirm that the couple had returned at some point. When the intern who accompanied me wanted to process what she had seen as well, I acted like I didn't know what she meant. It would be days before I could speak about it, and even then, only with a few close friends.

I had seen something I couldn't deny, and I now had two choices: step up and get my questions answered or step down and bury my head. Was I willing to learn more about what I had seen? I started with what I believed was true. I knew the Devil was real because I read my Bible. He had fallen angels called demons in his army. Because of how it had moved and responded to the name of Jesus, I didn't think it was an angel. I knew evil was real because I had faced temptation and felt darkness before. But I still had plenty of gaps to fill in.

Even with all the verses in the Bible, the subject of Satan and his spiritual warfare can be hard to put our theological fingers on. How can we, as Christians, become more fluent in this topic? What is the Enemy's role in our lives? How much access does he have to us? How much power do I have over him? The Bible says God came to destroy the Devil's work, so what exactly is he working on then?

The questions kept coming: How can we learn about the Devil without giving him undue attention? Can we grow discernment like a muscle, working it out until this muscle is strong enough to carry us through whatever situation we find ourselves in? If we learn his patterns, can we possibly predict him? And then, working within God's power, can we prevent his plan for our ruin instead of just looking to pick up the pieces afterward? Does he exploit our sin? Does he create circumstances where our weakness makes us vulnerable to sin? Does he push us? How can he be stopped? What does the Bible say?

The crazy experience that night activated a journey I've been taking in my spiritual life ever since. Never again would I turn away from the invisible truth surrounding my life: I have an enemy that seeks to harm me but a Protector who can equip me for battle. When I read my Bible, I see that God wants me to take a more proactive approach; He wants me to face the Enemy rather than tuck my tail and run in the other direction. He wants me to learn the power of shouting down the Devil with *No!*

To illustrate what I'm getting at, we are a sports family; my children play all year round. Sports teach discipline and teamwork, and they give us all a chance to cheer for others. It's been fun to watch our hometown in Ohio embrace a new professional soccer team, FC Cincinnati. So far, the team has seen record-breaking crowds and had amazing success. I went to my first game recently and watched a competitor drive the ball down the field and take an excellent shot at our goal. People were groaning around me, expecting the shot to succeed, when the goalie, Mitch, miraculously saved it at the last moment. Spontaneously, a chant arose: *"Mitch says no! Mitch says no! Mitch says no!"* I laughingly joined in with the crowd. The next time the other team shot at our goal, I felt prepared, and even eager, as we again gave credit to the goalie's skills. *Mitch says no!*

An unseen enemy is present in every conflict—stirring the pot, poking our bruises, whispering his lies to us. When there is brokenness, defeat, shame, and judgment, he is victorious. I am so sick of his success. I am staking a claim over my life and my household—not today, not me, not this marriage, not this house, not this day, no, no, no! *Beth says no.*

I am staking a claim over my life and my household.

And wouldn't it be amazing if people started cheering us on? *Mitch says no! Beth says no!* I have to think every time that goalie hears his name roared throughout the stadium, he experiences a rush of adrenaline to stop the ball again. What if we said more loudly than normal, when we see the Devil's handiwork, "No. Not today." What if my refrain was loud enough for you to hear and you joined me in that chorus? What if we looked like a tough opponent to that enemy, instead of an easy target? What skills would I need to develop to effectively fight Satan and his attempt to ruin my life?

The secret sauce isn't really that secret. While we say yes to Jesus, we say no to Satan. Yes, Jesus, I believe Your ways are best. I will forever be on this journey in pursuit of You. No, Satan, I see your traps and no matter how shiny they look, I will walk away. Both an offensive strategy and a defensive strategy are needed, and the first step is learning about the opponent: who he is, how he works, and where he strikes.

That night in the *bodega* wouldn't be the last time I came close to evil. Now that I was on to him, I called out the Enemy in tension-filled rooms and in prayer over friends with unexplained illnesses. I had a lot to learn, and I still do, but a decade later, I am ready to tell my stories of victory and defeat for the purpose of equipping the Church. This topic has often been relegated to the fringes of our faith communities, but I don't understand why. I think that's part of his schtick. He wants us to think he's *way* out there, when in reality, he's always nearby. I am sick of having polite conversations about "Christian topics" and meanwhile giving up ground to the Enemy without ever addressing the war we are in. I want each of us to know his limits and our own strengths through Christ.

My hope is for a Church alert to the spiritual battle and unafraid to advance against the kingdom of darkness. It has meant allowing God to expand my understanding of Him and what He can do, and it has meant losing some innocence in situations in which I would rather stay ignorant. But the payoff is huge: kingdom advancement, construction instead of destruction, strength instead of shame. Ultimately, we can have hope in any storyline we find ourselves in, because the story's ending has already been told.

Before we start, it may help to know that this book is divided into three sections. First we'll get familiar with what exactly is the spiritual battle. The second section, and majority of our time together, will be spent outlining the many tricks and tactics Satan uses to partner with our sin nature and create chaos. The third section is a final encouragement to understand the tools we've been given and a reminder to use them regularly. The more we understand what's happening around us, the more in step with the Spirit we become.

Along the way, I'll be introducing you to dozens of Hebrew words. I share them because they have become part of my offensive strategy—new understanding has led me to new boldness. God isn't impressed with my head knowledge; there's no vocabulary test to get into heaven. But He is watching how I live differently because of the new insight He's granted.

Part I

Destroying the Devil's Work

"The reason the Son of God appeared was to destroy the devil's work."
1 John 3:8

Chapter 1

He uses the same tricks over and over.

"I have given you authority to trample on snakes and scorpions and to overcome all the power of the enemy; nothing will harm you."
Luke 10:19

Once when our family was vacationing in Key West, I decided to splurge on a shark excursion. Aboard the boat, I was delighted by the sea air and thrilled to see something up close that I had previously only seen on TV. The crew poured ripped fish into the water and explained that the blood would draw the sharks near to the boat. Immediately, the sharks appeared behind the bow and feasted on the fish. We took pictures, fascinated to be near something so dangerous. At the time, we were living in Mexico, and my experience with dangerous animals was limited to the stray dogs in our neighborhood. I would carry rocks in my hand when I went running and preemptively throw them when I felt threatened. It made me feel powerful to know I was sending the message *don't mess with me, dogs*, even if they were already planning on letting me run by.

Watching the sharks devour the bloody fish, a thought entered my mind. *This must be what the Smith family feels like.* We loved the Smiths, who I imagined felt just like those fish. They had experienced an unexpected tragedy, and instead of being left alone to heal, things were going from bad to worse: a child struggling with the injustice of life and turning to drugs; their marriage straining under the pressure and loss; bodies breaking down under stress; everything costing time, money, sleep, and margin. They were metaphorically bleeding in the water as the sharks continued to circle.

This is how the Enemy works. He is drawn to blood. When he sees a body breaking down, he doubles down and attacks the marriage or the mind. He doesn't leave us alone when we are bleeding, off to attack something healthy. Instead, he sees a chance for possible total destruction. Injury—whether physical, relational, emotional, or spiritual—attracts him.

Satan uses the same tricks over and over and over again. There are no original stories. He uses sex, money, pride. He uses deceit, selfishness, anxiety. We can read throughout both Testaments stories of everyday people who didn't understand the deception they were under. The combination of our own weakness (within), the world (around), and the Devil (nearby) creates havoc and derails God's plans for our lives. If we'll keep our eyes open for Satan, we'll become more comfortable wading into the dark and turning on the light. He is counting on us being scared of the dark, or being afraid that in some way another person's pain is contagious, so we don't linger. I get most tired or discouraged when I think it's up to me to save someone or something. I've made this rookie mistake more times than I want to recount. I was certain if *I* didn't do something, all would be lost. I now know better: there is only one shelter to rest under, and there is only one Savior who died on a cross. Anything I offer, I do so as His ambassador. He does the prompting, calling, empowering, rescuing, and saving.

Anything I offer, I do so as His ambassador.

Jesus forgives, directs, comforts. He provides answers, He convicts. This is all His job. I can step into a role that isn't mine far too easily, especially when someone willingly puts me there. But I won't do it again; the consequences are grave. Hard stories should draw us to Jesus, not to man. We are at our best when we continually reinforce this truth. I can want to give someone something or meet a need only God can, but doing so ends up making the story messier. Whether I am frustrated with a chapter of a story I'm invested in or unhappy with the timing of something, I have no choice but to rest in the truth that He is sovereign. It's the evidence of a powerful faith: trust Him and His timing. If He allowed it, He has a purpose for it. If something or someone isn't moving on our timetable, we can trust God, who has a better perspective; He is working on what we cannot see. The peace I crave sits on top of this truth: He is in control.

Witnessing the struggles of our friends the Smiths was the first time I remember being weary of putting on my spiritual armor and waiting for the Devil to attack, hoping the belt or the helmet was in place. Why did he get to go first? What would a *counterattack* look like? What kind of repellent is out there, or what first punch could I throw that would scare the sharks away like my rock throwing did for the dogs?

In the biblical story of Job, we see a blatant attempt to dissuade him of God's faithfulness. Satan attacks various parts of Job's life, watching for which blow will be fatal to his faith. Job stands strong, but there are casualties. In hindsight we can read it, cheering Job on, grieving what he's lost, understanding it's a war and he's just a pawn in it. But the rivals are unequally matched, and ultimately, God wins and Job's life is restored. Through this old story, we learn that although the world God created is good, it's not always safe.

Some of the not-perfect-and-unsafe is a result of living in a fallen world. We get sick or people die, and it's not fair. Some suffering is because we sin or others sin, and the consequences are destruction, conflict, loss, and brokenness. And finally, some of the hard we experience is designed by an enemy, our adversary, who is relentlessly on the attack. Knowing this to be true, could we live a life where we take new spiritual ground, rather than just hold him back or fight him off? What if I put on my gloves and throw the first punch? What if I become so adept at offensive fighting that God asks me to step into the ring and fight for others?

Have you ever asked yourself, *How did it get this bad?* The Smiths did. As they sat with Todd and me and we reflected on the trajectory of their fall and all the people who had been hurt, I muttered to myself, "Damn Devil." Todd looked over at me, half amused, half shocked, and asked what I meant. I explained, "I am so mad at the Devil. He saw an opening and dove in. This is *such* an old story, we should have seen it coming." Their story involved sexual sin, which is as old as Genesis. How much more do we need to see or read to understand the Devil loves to pervert? What if we asked ourselves *before* temptation, *I wonder how the Enemy might try to get in?* Then we stand guard at that door, and maybe even at each other's doors.

There's no denying Satan wants as much mileage as he can get from a sin choice on my part, or a hard situation I find myself in. If I make a poor decision and sin, natural consequences occur for that sin. Like the hungry shark, when he senses weakness, the Enemy circles around, looking for a place to come in. When I'm left bleeding a bit, he comes and feasts on my shame or my despair or the rift it puts in my relationships. Ephesians 4:27 admonishes, "Do not give the devil a foothold," literally a place where he can stand or walk securely. Left unattended, a foothold gives him room to settle in and create a stronghold. It's at this point I end up asking, "How did it get this bad?" I want there to be no place the Enemy can hold on to me.

The Devil is a double-downer and leaves a wake of hard stories wherever he attacks—people in chaos and in need of God's peace and intervention. However, as strong and dark as the Enemy can appear, Exodus 8:19 teaches there is more power in even the "finger of God."

My friend Stephanie was going through a hard season, the kind with no end in sight and no easy answers. Not knowing what to do or say, and unable to fix anything, I was tempted to avoid her. But as a Christian, I shouldn't want to disconnect from her. I can be in proximity to pain because the Bible tells me what to do with it. In the book of Exodus, God instructs Moses to build a tabernacle. Basically, the instructions are to make room for God, and He will come and fill the space (Ex. 25).

That's my opportunity with Steph: make room for God in our conversations, in her lament, in my listening, and He'll come. If she needs protection, strength, peace ... it's not up to me to give it to her; He'll do it. My role is to come near and hold her hands, and we've now created twice the space for God to fill. In that space, I can ask the question, "If I were the Enemy, what would I want to happen next? What would be victory for him?" Then I know where to be looking for the next attack and how I can fight. It feels ridiculously good not to be waiting for the shoe to drop, but to counterpunch with spiritual weapons.

I've admittedly experienced a steep growth curve while becoming involved in hard stories like those of the Smiths and Steph. I tend to wrestle with wanting to see something or someone who is broken become unbroken, and so I will dedicate energy toward putting him or her back together. I'll expend emotional energy on why or who broke the person or relationship in the first place. But God is teaching me we can't fix what He wants to heal. When I try to fix something—or worse yet, someone—I usually cover up or distract from what God wants to do in that person or me. When He heals, the result is stronger and the impact greater.

The mark of fluency in hard stories is the confidence that God has not forgotten the people we are called to love. He doesn't wring His hands, and He doesn't want us to tap out. His work is a long play. Our culture begs for instant gratification, and I can be guilty of thinking, *Why isn't this getting easier or the situation improving?* However, faith is much like a muscle. The more I exercise, the stronger I am. I can be tempted to give up, but people are always worth the effort and the trials. If God is asking me to engage, He'll strengthen me for the task. And in the way only He can, He'll use it to increase my faith as well. While I am busy with worrying, *Will this ever get better? What will happen next? Can they handle it?*, God is sitting on His throne, privy to the whole story and perfect in His timing. That was His point in asking Job at the end of the book (Job 38):

> "Where were you when I laid the foundation of the earth?" (v. 4 NASB).
>
> "Have you ever in your life commanded the morning?" (v. 12 NASB).
>
> "What is the way to the abode of light? And where does darkness reside?" (v. 19).
>
> "Can you bring forth the constellations in their seasons?" (v. 32).

In response to these questions, Job answered, "Behold, I am insignificant; what can I say in response to You? I put my hand on my mouth. I have spoken once, and I will not reply; or twice, and I will add nothing more" (Job 40:3–5 NASB).

Among the Enemy's bag of tricks is to hide behind attacks of isolation, temptation, and shame. If we don't see him, don't believe he exists, or don't understand his tactics, he gets twice the mileage. His pattern is to attack and create chaos, and we blame ourselves for it. God never leaves us, and we can read lots of Scripture about how His eyes are always on us. However, we can try to hide from *Him*. We can also not call on Him out of shame, when He is the very and only Person who can save us. I used to think the goal was to outrun the Devil with good choices; just stay on the path, and he can't touch you. But looking back, I realize those messages came from people trying to convince me to live well. And while blessings follow obedience, it falsely leads me to believe if I just do what I am "supposed" to, evil will leave me alone. That's first of all not true and, secondly, prevents me from joining God in "destroy[ing] the devil's work" (1 John 3:8).

If we don't see the Enemy, don't believe he exists, or don't understand his tactics, he gets twice the mileage.

In the same way that Jesus asks us to partner with Him to advance the gospel by putting God's ways and love on display, we can unintentionally partner with the Devil and advance his purposes of division, rebellion, shame, etc. However, when we acknowledge the reality of evil, when we stop seeing the Devil as a caricature or a cartoon, then we truly understand his utter bent on our destruction. "He was a murderer from the beginning, not holding to the truth, for there is no truth in him" (John 8:44).

One night, Todd and I were sitting on the front porch of our home. It had been a tough week, and he was leaving the next day for India, where the ministry we serve, Back2Back, cares for orphans. It felt like we were being attacked—physically, relationally, spiritually, financially—and I didn't want him to leave. I told Todd, "Remember that military campaign in Iraq, Operation Shock and Awe? That's what this feels like. The Devil has decided to attack via land, air, and sea."

I was almost pouting. "I don't want you to leave. I know 'He that is in me is greater than he that is in the world,' but still … it's more fun to fight alongside you." We talked and prayed, and I eventually capitulated. I knew I would be fine and he should fulfill his commitment to travel.

The next day I looked for a Bible verse I had heard somewhere. All I remembered were a few words: "nothing will harm you." After a quick search, I found Luke 10:19, "I have given you authority to trample on snakes and scorpions and to overcome all the power of the enemy; nothing will harm you." I wrote it on a note card and carried it in my pocket all day. I shared it with my children and fell asleep with it next to my bed. It takes twenty-four hours to travel to India, so I had yet to hear from Todd.

I woke up the next morning to a text message with an accompanying video from Todd. I sat up to watch it and was shocked to see a king cobra right outside of the ministry campus. Todd's text explained that the man in the video was a snake catcher. He was demonstrating how he could control the snake with a tiny rock in his hands. When he showed it to the snake, it slithered back into its bag, as if intimidated by the rock. When he put it out of sight, the snake emerged, emboldened and ready to escape. Several times he showed how the little pebble controlled the snake's movement.

Todd's text message read, "The little rock is a piece of snake cartilage. Apparently they are afraid of it and snake catchers use it to their advantage. I was thinking about our week and the snake that seemed loose in our garden. The rock we have is the name of Jesus. It seems small, but when pulled out, the snake has to go back in the bag, fully controlled." Todd didn't know that the day before, I had been reading the verse about having authority to trample snakes, but God did. He was sending me a powerful message about not being afraid and understanding the tools He has put in *my* hand.

I still had plenty of questions about these tools: How do I use them? When do I use them? Is the Devil behind every disappointment and setback, or is some of it just my own sin nature? Can we predict his next move? Can we be preemptive and protective, instead of reactive and silent? What are his favorite tricks and how might we recognize them? How then can we appropriately assign blame to him instead of attacking each other? I have been trying to ask before every meeting, every conversation, every day: What is happening here that I cannot see? How might the Enemy want to advance? How can I frustrate his plans instead of cooperate with him?

These are the questions I've been exploring as I long to partner with God in dismantling the kingdom of darkness. If I am to look like Him, then I want to learn how to get good at demolishing the Devil's work. The answer always starts with confession.

"The reason the Son of God appeared was to destroy the devil's work" (1 John 3:8).

What questions do you have about evil or enemy activity?

Are you more spiritually comfortable on defense or offense? Why?

What tricks has the Enemy used on you (over and over again)?

Chapter 2

He can't win.

The joke is on him.

"Therefore, this is what the LORD says: 'If you return, then I will restore you—you will stand before Me; and if you extract the precious from the worthless, you will become My spokesman.'"

Jeremiah 15:19 NASB

One night I received a frantic call from a dear friend. "My son is telling me something crazy, and I don't understand it. Can I bring him over and have him share it with you?" After the seventeen-year-old boy and his parents were made comfortable in my living room, he spoke shakily with downcast eyes, "I have been thinking some really terrible thoughts—pornographic, violent thoughts—not what you might imagine." He stumbled over his words, red-faced and ashamed. "It started when I was young, and they aren't pleasurable, they are … *filthy*." He looked up at me, desperate for understanding.

I didn't know what he was facing, but I sensed it was dark and powerful. This was war, and the only appropriate response was to make room for God and ask Him to use us to destroy the Devil's work.

"Let's pray. I'll get Todd involved, and your parents are here … Let's just pray around you for a while and see what the Lord reveals." I paused, wanting to ascertain his level of buy-in to what I anticipated the evening would hold. "Tell me, in sharing this, what were you hoping for?"

His single-word response made my hair stand on end. *"Freedom."*

I grabbed my Bible, and he sat in a chair as we all began to pray. I laid my hands on his back, and as soon as I did, *my* mind was filled with a horrific, pornographic image. I pulled my hand away as if I had been burned. "Oh, wow," I said compassionately, as understanding filled me. "If what I just saw was a glimpse into your world, I am *so sorry*. God allowed me to see what you are facing—for sure this is demonic."

Along with his parents, we spent the next several hours praying over him, singing worship songs, and reading Scripture. I didn't have much experience in this kind of spiritual fight. It felt heavy, and I sensed we would somehow know when a knockout blow was dealt. In the beginning of our time with the young man, the Lord gave me a picture of a tree being cut down. I told him regarding this battle, "When you cut down a tree, it doesn't fall with one strike. You have to keep at it and weaken it until it drops. We won't give up or stop until it's over." I knew in some biblical stories relief and deliverance came with one word, but other times Jesus said it would take prayer and fasting (Mark 9:29).

Sitting in that room, admittedly in some new spiritual territory, I reminded myself of a couple of things:

- Jesus is the star of the story. (People cannot take credit for what only God can do.)
- God's truth is torture to evil. Read Scripture to be sure war is being waged.
- God inhabits the praises of His people, so sing when darkness overwhelms.
- God wants us free, so we are in His will when we ask for release from evil.

Armed with these assurances and in the presence of fellow Jesus warriors, we kept at it, sometimes having to hold him down, until finally, he leaned over and vomited. Afterward, he sat up and sighed. "I am free." We were all exhausted; not only was it the middle of the night, but we had been through a battle. Nevertheless, he jumped out of the chair with new enthusiasm and ran around the small room. "Baptize me! Baptize me now!" he commanded.

A little later we gathered around their backyard pool. I watched him go down and then come up by the light of the moon, and I heard his shouts of pure joy, evidence he was feeling spiritually free.

That night I lay in bed. *What just happened? What was that?* Todd and I weren't from a charismatic background; no one "taught" us to do what happened that night—it just unfolded. I had so many questions: Is all pornography demonic? If this young man was a Christ follower before this evening, how had he been so tortured? Did his relief come from his mustard seed of faith, or ours? I opened my Bible and read all I could from the first five books of the New Testament, finding many versions of what I had experienced that night. What did Jesus do when confronted with stories like these, and what did His disciples model for us? Why don't we talk about demons? Who can I share this with? Will people think it is strange?

The joke was absolutely on the Enemy. I'm sure what happened next made him regret who he had picked on. The young man's parents immediately entered into full-time ministry, studying all they could about what we had seen that night. The young man grew up to testify regularly how God freed him. And I set off on a journey to understand this world I could not see but now thoroughly believed existed.

It was painful to witness this young man experience that kind of unseen torture, but here were the ultimate results:

- transparency and relationship were cemented between parent and child, and between parents;
- unleashing of ministry in this family;
- biblical curiosity on my part;
- baptism of a young man;
- and the impact continues as I share this story with you.

We tend to see only what's hard or focus on a losing score or an eminent defeat. A big part of maturation in Christ is understanding God's sovereignty and reminding ourselves and each other: this is a long story. We must have each other's backs. God always triumphs over the intention of evil and turns it around for His purpose.

A big part of maturation in Christ is understanding God's sovereignty and reminding ourselves and each other: this is a long story.

If we are distracted by worry, selfishness, pride, and lust, then we are broken and ashamed. If I go about my day, oblivious to what the Enemy is doing, I am no threat. If I choose comfort over conflict, I am not advancing anything other than my own agenda. Turns out, God gave me a role in this spiritual war. I am not a pawn, I have a voice, and that voice can declare God is sovereign and we are victorious. When I use the power God gives me, His kingdom advances. I am not somewhere holding the line, bracing for an attack. I am moving boldly and unharmed, "among the fiercest powers of darkness, trampling every one of them beneath your feet!" (Ps. 91:13 TPT). Satan hates God, and since we are God's kids, he's willing to get to God by hurting us. What if instead of trying to outrun him, or hide from him, or ignore him, I look evil in the face and say, "I will war with you before I allow any ground to be taken"?

Once when we were in Israel, we learned about an ancient game fought in the arenas of the Roman Empire. The orchestrators would chain two gladiators together and then release a wild animal against them. If they could work together, they would defeat the animal every time. However, if they allowed doubt in the other or pride to come between them, the animal would win. In the same way, I have an enemy who is looking to come between me and whomever I am with. When we work against each other, he wins. But when we fight together, he doesn't stand a chance.

God is relational—within His trinity and with us, His creation. Since we are made in His image, we, too, are relationship-dependent, made to flourish in community. It's why the Enemy so viciously attacks our interpersonal connections with one another. God understands the battles are fierce, and He gives us people to fight alongside.

Jeremiah wrote about extracting the precious from the worthless: "Therefore, this is what the LORD says: 'If you return, then I will restore you—you will stand before Me; and if you extract the precious from the worthless, you will become My spokesman'" (Jer. 15:19 NASB). In our relationships, we need conversations of substance, authenticity, inconvenience … people who ask hard questions, who show up, and who say, *You are worth it.*

Who fights alongside you?

Which of the three tools are you most comfortable with (prayer, Scripture, or praise)?

Have you seen deliverance in your life? Was it initiated through repentance, or through prayer?

Chapter 3

God has the real power.

"Yet all the Israelites had light in the places where they lived."
Exodus 10:23

It was nice outside, so we had the top down on the convertible as I drove my son Josh home from a doctor's appointment. As we came to a stop at an intersection, we heard a sidewalk evangelist shouting verses and admonitions through a bullhorn. I tuned out his abrasive approach, until he caught my attention when he yelled, "If you go to one of this city's megachurches, be warned! They will not teach you about Satan, our real enemy. They only want you to feel good and safe, but *you are not!*" I looked over at him and smiled. He had no idea he was speaking to the interim pastor of one of those megachurches. Although I didn't build that house, at the moment it was under my leadership.

Josh pleaded with me not to pull over, so we drove on, but the preacher's words stuck with me all afternoon. *Do we talk enough about Satan in the church? What do we know about him? What does it mean that God created him? The more we know about our adversary, the more effectively we can fight him.*

What does the Bible tell us? The prophets Isaiah and Ezekiel give us some insight into who the Enemy is. We learn he was in heaven and fell—cast down. He was arrogant and prideful, and now lives in the pit.

How you have fallen from heaven,
   morning star,* son of the dawn!
You have been cast down to the earth,
   you who once laid low the nations!
You said in your heart,
   "I will ascend to the heavens;
I will raise my throne
   above the stars of God;
I will sit enthroned on the mount of assembly,
   on the utmost heights of Mount Zaphon.
I will ascend above the tops of the clouds;
   I will make myself like the Most High."
But you are brought down to the realm of the dead,
   to the depths of the pit. (Isa. 14:12–15)

Consider these facts we learn about our enemy directly from Scripture:

- He has many names; "Satan" occurs fifty-three times in the Bible and is best translated as "adversary." This accurately describes him—a rival of God and His kids. Satan is against us and wants our utter destruction.
- He transforms himself into an "angel of light" (2 Cor. 11:14), disguising himself to further deceive.
- Peter described him as our "enemy" and the "devil" (1 Pet. 5:8). The Greek word for *devil* is *diabolos*, meaning "defamer" or "slanderer." He whispers lies and maligns us, desiring God's kids to feel and experience misery.

---

* Interestingly, the "morning star" from verse 12 is sometimes translated as "Lucifer" (meaning "light bearer" or "light bringer"), but it's a Latin word, not a Hebrew one. This is its only representation in Scripture, and its story is long and debatable, so for our purposes we won't use this name for our enemy.

- Satan is depicted as the "ruler of this world" (John 12:31; 14:30; 16:11 NASB) and "the god of this age" (2 Cor. 4:4), but he doesn't have legitimate authority. I've had moments when I insisted I had authority *over him* as a co-heir with Christ.
- He's called the "evil one" (1 John 5:18–19).
- He's the "prince of the power of the air" (Eph. 2:2 KJV). The verse continues, "the spirit who is now at work in those who are disobedient." "Working" in the Greek is *energeo*, which means "to energize, to be active, to be at work." It is in the present, continuous tense, reinforcing that our enemy is constantly operating against us. He is energizing the human spirit within those who are disobedient.
- Satan is the prince of a hellish army and deploys them to torture, tempt, and oppress. He roams and hunts (Job 1:7; 1 Pet. 5:8) and sends his fallen angels to do his bidding. He isn't omnipresent—everywhere at the same time. Only God is omnipresent (Ps. 121:3; Prov. 15:3).

It's important to remember who our enemy is and where he came from. Satan was beautiful, ordained, anointed, and blameless until wickedness was found in him. Evil can dress up in pretty clothes and call to us, but he is violent and sinful, prideful and corrupt.

> The word of the LORD came to me: "Son of man, take up a lament concerning the king of Tyre and say to him: 'This is what the Sovereign LORD says:
>
> "'You were the seal of perfection,
>   full of wisdom and perfect in beauty.

You were in Eden,
> the garden of God;
every precious stone adorned you:
>> carnelian, chrysolite and emerald,
>> topaz, onyx and jasper,
>> lapis lazuli, turquoise and beryl.
Your settings and mountings were made of gold;
> on the day you were created they were prepared.
You were anointed as a guardian cherub,
> for so I ordained you.
You were on the holy mount of God;
> you walked among the fiery stones.
You were blameless in your ways
> from the day you were created
> till wickedness was found in you.
Through your widespread trade
> you were filled with violence,
> and you sinned.
So I drove you in disgrace from the mount of God,
> and I expelled you, guardian cherub,
> from among the fiery stones.
Your heart became proud
> on account of your beauty,
and you corrupted your wisdom
> because of your splendor.
So I threw you to the earth;
> I made a spectacle of you before kings.'"""
>> (Ezek. 28:11–17)

He knows how to be attractive and he is intelligent, but we have his playbook. He just does the same things over and over. The Bible calls him "the devil" and "Satan," "the deceiver of the whole world" … "the accuser." Since every story is an old one, we know how it can end. Friends misunderstanding each other? Marriages strained under pressure? Temptation leading to addiction? Rebellious children? Churches splitting? Lust twisting to perversion? There's only so many ways you can rearrange our sin. We see these same patterns in Scripture and can learn from them how Satan will strike. He's actually pretty predictable: Temptation is the beckoning finger of our accuser luring us to walk into traps that are ultimately designed to hurt us. He will look for our weakness, then bite. Afterward, he attacks where we are wounded until the fight is drained out of us.

> Temptation is the beckoning finger of our accuser luring us to walk into traps that are ultimately designed to hurt us.

These ancient biblical stories of deception and evil frame all the stories we find ourselves in today. Because of Satan, we have sin and need the redeeming work of Jesus on the cross. His resurrection conquered all sin and demonstrated victory over this defeated enemy. A quick look at current events through the lens of good and evil shows Satan on the prowl: rioting in cities is rooted in Satan; foreign dictators starving their people is rooted in Satan. Every crime story, every war story, every broken piece of this world points to the Enemy and the wickedness found in him. If that's true, then I don't want to put bandages on problems, but rather fight to get to the root of the issue. Spiritual battles can't be fought with human solutions; if we can learn to put on our spiritual glasses, we will see things as they really are.

Church historian Theodoret recorded a true story about the Asian monk Telemachus, who lived in the Roman Empire. One day Telemachus awakened with a prophetic call to walk to Rome, although he didn't know why. When he arrived, for the first time he saw the spectacular gladiator games. He couldn't believe what he was seeing: humans fighting each other to the death, crowds of tens of thousands cheering when blood was spilled—murder as entertainment. He looked with spiritual eyes and saw it as evil rather than cultural. Wanting it to stop, this diminutive monk made his way out onto the arena sand. There are two accounts told of how he died that day in AD 391. Some say he was immediately put to death by a gladiator. Others submit that the crowd threw goblets and fruit at him, angry he had stopped their show, and he was essentially stoned to death. Either way, historians agree that he died quickly and the entire crowd left in silence.

Roman Emperor Honorius, impressed with Telemachus's martyrdom, promptly issued a historic ban on gladiatorial fights.[1] This terrible evil, which the Enemy was getting plenty of mileage from (death of a person, fear in the slaves, appetite for violence in the crowd, gambling, etc.), ceased because one man was willing to stand up. He died for his stand, but imagine his welcome into heaven!

We don't have gladiatorial games in our culture today, but we do have violence as entertainment; we have fear and senseless killings. We have circumstances where the Enemy has gained an advantage and God is looking to partner with His children to make it stop. This idea of spiritual warfare impacts our personal lives in our families, marriages, households, and friendships, but it also involves large, systemic strongholds.

Telemachus was bold but not unique. God has used boys and girls to stand up to giants, and old men to face off against ruthless leaders, since the Old Testament. One of my favorite passages in the Bible is the story of Moses and the plagues. The powerful Pharaoh, who had enslaved God's people for hundreds of years, was given the chance to do right and let the people go free. As he stalled and denied their requests, God sent ten plagues to get his attention. Those plagues weren't random; they each corresponded to a specific demonstration of evil in Egyptian culture. The Egyptians had a god of the Nile, so a plague turned the Nile into blood. Their god of fertility possessed the head of a frog, so God sent the plague of the frogs. Their god of creation's head resembled a fly's, hence the plague of the flies. Every plague corresponded to directly attack the strength Pharaoh and his people believed was theirs. (I wonder, if plagues were sent to our culture today, what would they attack?)

I love studying all the plagues, but I am captivated by the plague of darkness.

> Then the LORD said to Moses, "Stretch out your hand toward the sky so that darkness spreads over Egypt— darkness that can be felt." So Moses stretched out his hand toward the sky, and total darkness covered all Egypt for three days. No one could see anyone else or move about for three days. Yet all the Israelites had light in the places where they lived. (Ex. 10:21–23)

I have been in darkness so thick you could feel it; it can seem like you can't move around in it. Our enemy loves the shadows; it's where fear, anger, lust, and any number of sins can fall—whether on a person or a place. Yet in verse 23 it says where God's people were, they had light among them. We can move in confidence in dark places; we don't have anything to fear. We may be outnumbered, lost, or overwhelmed, but still, He's reaching for us.

Returning to the story of Telemachus: the Romans had been watching death all day. Why did his death have any impact on them? When he stood up for what was right, the winds changed. I've seen it before in other settings. I think with his sacrifice, God began to move in the spiritual realm.

The word for *wind* in Hebrew is *ruah*, the same as *spirit*. To me, Hebrew words are like doorknobs: when turned, they take you into new rooms of understanding. It's not necessary to know how to say the words, or even remember how to spell them. What is important is how we live differently because we've been in those new rooms. While on a walk, I taught the word *ruah* to my four-year-old granddaughter. She liked saying it and how it delighted me when she did. Several days later, we were playing hide-and-seek in the yard and it was getting dark, so I told her we would need to head inside. "But it's okay, because I can still feel the *ruah*," she told me. She was living differently—with boldness—because of her understanding that the Spirit was with her.

I've been in meetings where I couldn't put my finger on why, but the tension felt unnecessarily thick. I have walked in parking lots where I had nothing to fear, but it still swept over me. We must be aware that otherworldly activity is around us. We can ask God for spiritual antennas to be sensitive to what is happening that we cannot see, because He will provide the means to combat it—and the boldness of His *ruah*.

One time we were dedicating a new ministry campus where horrific activity had previously occurred. During the worship service, for no reason, the transformer blew and the power went out, but the people who had gathered kept singing. Then a strong wind swept through and we sensed the Spirit was with us. We finished the prayer service by candlelight, and in the morning, everyone was stunned to see damage to the cinder blocks in the second story of the building that looked like the result of a punch, as if for a moment the wrestling in the heavenly territory had broken through.

A terrifying image depicted in Egyptian art from the time of Moses is of Pharaoh holding helpless people by their hair with his right hand, extending that same right arm as a symbol of his power over the people. That outstretched arm was intended to intimidate or dominate the people he was suppressing.

To counter for His people, God promised that with His own "outstretched arm" He would redeem them (Ex. 6:6) and "by the power of [His] arm they will be as still as a stone" (15:16). In fact, more than two dozen times, He commanded similarly to "go tell the Egyptians, I'll bring them out by my arm." After the final plague and their release, the Israelites rushed to the Red Sea, and God instructed Moses to "stretch out your hand" (14:21, 26–27). It was as if God was saying, "You want to see what real power is? Watch this: I'll use My arm not to crush you, but to save you."

He was foreshadowing what would later be prophesied in Isaiah 53:1–6:

> Who has believed our message
>   and to whom has the arm of the LORD been revealed?
> He grew up before him like a tender shoot,
>   and like a root out of dry ground.
> He had no beauty or majesty to attract us to him,
>   nothing in his appearance that we should desire him.
> He was despised and rejected by mankind,
>   a man of suffering, and familiar with pain.
> Like one from whom people hide their faces
>   he was despised, and we held him in low esteem.
>
> Surely he took up our pain
>   and bore our suffering,
> yet we considered him punished by God,
>   stricken by him, and afflicted.
> But he was pierced for our transgressions,
>   he was crushed for our iniquities;
> the punishment that brought us peace was on him,
>   and by his wounds we are healed.

We all, like sheep, have gone astray,

    each of us has turned to our own way;

and the LORD has laid on him

    the iniquity of us all.

God's arm carried the sin of the world, and that's *real* power. Because God reached for us, we can face armies and know He is always with us. We can experience victory over sin that threatens our lives. We can sit in the darkness and find peace. We can be in a chapter of a hard story we don't like and know, *it's not over yet.*

Do we talk enough about Satan in the Church?

What do we know about him?

What does Telemachus's testimony teach us?

Have you been in darkness so thick you could feel it? What was your response?

Chapter 4

When it looks like we're surrounded, we're surrounded by Him.

"Then the LORD opened the servant's eyes, and he looked and saw the hills full of horses and chariots of fire all around Elisha."
2 Kings 6:17

Meme was a woman who lived with Todd and me throughout our fifteen missionary years in Mexico. She was like a Mexican grandmother to our children. Orphaned as a baby and then eventually widowed, she was a caregiver in a children's home when we first met her. Her view of life was simple: love others, as Jesus loves you. When we returned to serve in the US office, she spent half the year with us and the other half in Mexico. While stateside, she fell in love with snow, chili dogs, American football, and the changing of the leaves. I've written about her before, as she taught me many lessons on poverty, service, forgiveness, and resilience.

In May of 2019, she developed a cough from a sickness commonly known as valley fever. In July, she came to the US for treatment and fought for her life under the very best medical care. In October, she was hospitalized for the third time, and we faced the reality that she was losing the fight and heaven was imminent. I remember telling her the doctors had done everything they could, and she was going to sing on streets of gold sooner than we imagined. As someone who was semi-literate, she learned many truths about God through worship songs, and she usually had earbuds in as she went about her day, singing to herself and the Lord.

On the day she died, a nurse came in to do a mental-fitness check, asking her the year and the name of the US president. When she couldn't answer, her eyes open but not totally *there*, the nurse pressed for her to say either my name or hers. Meme was still unable to answer. The nurse shook her head at us as she backed out of the room and said, "It won't be much longer."

Saddened to be at the end of this fight—out of emotional and medical options—I curled up at the foot of her hospital bed and sang a worship song to her. "*Sumérgeme*" ("Submerge Me") describes being tired and washed in the river of God's Spirit, which seemed to fit our circumstances and was a longtime favorite of hers. We'd sung it for two decades when facing bad storms, difficult children, and other threats. I could see from her eyes that she recognized me and what I was singing.

As I choked out the first verse, I thought about the spiritual tool worship is for us. Psalm 22:3 talks about how God inhabits the praises of His people, and singing in that moment of big, hard feelings, I could feel Him with us. When I began the chorus, to my surprise she chimed in—her only words of the day. Tears in my eyes, I looked over to Todd incredulously. *Where does worship go inside of you … that when you don't even know your own name, you don't forget His?*

Ahavah is a Hebrew word meaning "to love." What fascinates me about *ahavah* is the root word *ahav*, which means "to give." Embedded in this idea of loving is giving. The way we show our love is by giving ourselves to the object of our affection.

The Bible is full of examples of this. We see a heavenly Father who loved so much that He gave us His only Son. We hear Paul teaching the early church how to practically show love to each other and put God on display.

We read Old Testament accounts of sacrificial parents and generous leaders. This is clearly a God idea—to love is to give.

God tells us we are to love our family, friends, and the foreigner. We are to love the lost, the least of these, our enemies, and our neighbors. "Jesus replied: "'Love the Lord your God with all your heart and with all your soul and with all your mind.' This is the first and greatest commandment. And the second is like it: 'Love your neighbor as *yourself*'" (Matt. 22:37–39).

What we have to give, we first get from Him. It might seem like others have bigger capacities to give or love, but they've simply learned how to tap into the Father's unlimited supply. If people listen well, they've been heard by God. If they encourage or are generous, they've received what they needed from Him. What I saw in Meme over the years came from her connection with the Spirit, who has an unending measure of all we need.

We can give time, advocacy, forgiveness, grace, encouragement, tangible needs, compassion, empathy, prayer, and the list goes on. We have been given much, and it's God's idea that we turn around and love others from our full hearts. The result will be a community that looks more like a kingdom of heaven on earth, so when people interact with any of us, they will feel more loved, more seen, more known. The hope is to be more mindful of opportunities for sacrifice and the chance to put action to our feelings. The outcome is a revolution, because loving well creates change, both in the giver and in the recipient. I am different because I loved Meme well and she loved me. This kind of loving makes the Enemy crazy, because we are overriding our natural selves to live supernaturally.

I was teaching about *ahavah* in a group setting when a man shared that he had attended a Jewish wedding that year. The rabbi taught that when you say *ahavah*, you hold out the last syllable, "ah," for as long as you can. It symbolizes we are to love and give until we are literally out of breath.

In that hospital room, the Enemy wasn't sitting back, watching this scene without regard. He was busy trying to stir up as much trouble as he could, wanting conflict, distrust, fear, and confusion to be left in the wake of Meme's departure. There were questions about transporting her body, concerns about finances, and a sense of loss among our children. There were hard conversations with her extended family and a general frustration that things didn't just turn around. This is always his mission. "The thief comes only to steal and kill and destroy; I have come that they may have life, and have it to the full" (John 10:10).

However, when faced with our biggest threat, death, God surrounded us with His presence and Meme went home to be with Jesus, accompanied by His peace. We can be in the middle of the most despairing of circumstances, and God will not leave us alone with the Devil. Like a bully facing his target, unaware the big brother is behind him, this enemy who comes after us is forced to acknowledge a much stronger and more powerful presence always has our backs. He tries using tactics of intimidation and fear so we feel alone, but as children of God, we carry Him within us. That is the power we need to still be in this war.

> ## We can be in the middle of the most despairing of circumstances, and God will not leave us alone with the Devil.

Consider this story of spiritual activity recorded in 2 Kings:

> Now the king of Aram was at war with Israel....
>
> The man of God sent word to the king of Israel: "Beware of passing that place, because the Arameans are going down there." So the king of Israel checked on the place indicated

by the man of God. Time and again Elisha warned the king, so that he was on his guard in such places.

This enraged the king of Aram. He summoned his officers and demanded of them, "Tell me! Which of us is on the side of the king of Israel?"

"None of us, my lord the king," said one of his officers, "but Elisha, the prophet who is in Israel, tells the king of Israel the very words you speak in your bedroom."

"Go, find out where he is," the king ordered, "so I can send men and capture him." The report came back: "He is in Dothan." Then he sent horses and chariots and a strong force there. They went by night and surrounded the city.

When the servant of the man of God got up and went out early the next morning, an army with horses and chariots had surrounded the city. "Oh no, my lord! What shall we do?" the servant asked.

"Don't be afraid," the prophet answered. "Those who are with us are more than those who are with them."

And Elisha prayed, "Open his eyes, LORD, so that he may see." Then the LORD opened the servant's eyes, and he looked and saw the hills full of horses and chariots of fire all around Elisha. (6:8–17)

If I could see the "hills" around me, how would it change how I walk through life? Psalm 68:17 says, "The chariots of God are myriads, thousands upon thousands" (NASB). Can I believe they have been dispatched to provide for and protect me as I engage in this cosmic battle? Would seeing those hills cause me to risk more? Engage more? Trust more?

Sin, the garden-variety kind I can conjure up alone, is what lures my eyes away from seeing myself in a long, old, powerful, spiritual story. Instead, sin pulls me into thinking what I really need I can get from Target or from special weekend plans. When I am focused on how I look to others or what I want to see occur, I lose spiritual power and authority. At that point, I am building my own kingdom, like I've let go of God's hand and don't need Him to do anything other than bless what I am busy about. He'll never let go of me, but I can step out of kingdom advancement when I turn my focus to my own self.

Like a hamster in a wheel, I realized that when a thought becomes almost obsessive, running around in my head, it's most likely not authored by God. I then found myself intrinsically motivated to avoid the consequences of runaway thoughts not centered on God. Lies lock down our minds, and we feel trapped, frozen, and stuck. They work us up, and we are the opposite of settled. On the other hand, truths flow in and out; they are free. They settle, even when they are hard. Once I could identify a sinful thought as a lie (even if it sounded like a familiar voice), I could walk through the confessional steps to get rid of it and be ready to battle the Enemy—not myself or someone else.

My relationship with admission of sin was rocky for a long time. I was, and still am, way more comfortable justifying my sin than confessing it. There always seems to be a good reason to say, do, or think what I am. Everything changed when I participated with some friends in a study where the focus was on sin confession. We would start by vulnerably sharing thoughts others couldn't see (sins like judgment, jealousy, lust), and the more we named ours, the less we paid attention to each other's. I felt such freedom to not have to posture myself to look good or try to control anyone else.

A couple of years later, I interviewed the author of that study, Rose Marie Miller, on my XM radio show. She and her husband founded World Harvest Mission, now rebranded as Serge. I asked her the motivation for writing the study, and she talked about her concern for missionaries they were sending into the field. She said, "I believe everyone has a spiritual Achilles' heel. My husband, Jack, and I wanted to help people identify theirs before the Devil surprises them and bites it."[2]

Missionaries aren't the only ones who have spiritual Achilles' heels. We all have storylines that trigger us and bring out our worst. The Enemy's role in my sinful choices is not in question. I sin because I am broken. As I shared the subject of this book with friends, they jokingly asked if I blamed the Devil for every pothole and fall. Of course not. Potholes result from the county's lack of attention to the roads, and I don't need the Devil to trip me; I fall just fine on my own. However, once we blow our tire in the pothole, or try to pick ourselves up from our fall, is the Enemy lying in wait, ready to take advantage? Absolutely. He is the Father of Lies and is hoping to get some mileage out of whatever hard situation we find ourselves in.

Here's how I've seen it work in my everyday life. I was on a walk with Todd, and we were talking about taking a few days away together. I *forgot* to ask, "If I were the Enemy, what would I want?" If I had, I might have been more cognizant of what happened next. It had been a heavy season, and I just wanted to get away. Todd had some expectations on where and for how long. (We like to say that expectations are like premeditated resentments.) The conversation should have been a lovely exchange, dreaming of rest and reconnection. But it started off on the wrong foot, and within minutes we were snapping at each other about how much we would spend, how long we would be gone, and how much work we'd take with us.

The Father of Lies was whispering in my ear, and I ate up those lies with a spoon. The tension between Todd and me was thick, and my sinful nature was on full display. I was manipulative, defensive, snarky, and self-righteous. Todd was on the offensive, prideful and demanding. We walked in silence for several minutes, having come to an impasse in our conversation.

By the end of the walk, I didn't want to go anywhere, at any time, with him. Then Todd wisely asked me in a quiet voice, "What does the Enemy gain from our conflict?" and I knew he was restarting the right conversation. I had been collaborating with the Enemy, and I needed to let go of my sin. Breakthrough begins with confession.

"I am sorry …" I responded to him, and confession opened the door for connection and spiritual victory. As I write this, I am on said vacation and having the time of my life. Damn the Devil; he has no authority over or with me.

Being mindful of the ever-constant spiritual battle brings me power. I am not subject to how the wind blows; I am a chief contributor to the story with God as the author by my side.

What worship songs do you have in your heart?

What have you given to and received from those you love?

Where in your life should you ask the question, "What does the Enemy want here?"

What is an example of a lie you have believed?

What's your relationship with confession been like?

Chapter 5

God isn't afraid of entering dark places.

"Praise be to the Lord, the God of Israel, because he
has come to his people and redeemed them."
Luke 1:68

My sister-in-law, Corrie, told the harrowing story of a time she was serving as a short-term missionary in a remote country, sharing the gospel in a dark place that was full of evil. The mission team was attempting to show a video portraying the story of Jesus, but the villagers were becoming increasingly aggressive, at one point lighting the Bibles they'd received on fire and throwing them at the screen.

Corrie's job was to stand with the equipment and pray. At one point when she looked up, she was surrounded by men and felt darkness. All the women and children had left, and there was a clear risk to the missionaries' lives. She bowed again to pray, and after a few moments she looked up when she heard a man speaking. He had some menacing dogs with him and was so intimidating that the village men had fled. He told the mission team to come with him to his family home in the hills. They instinctively knew they could trust him, so they accompanied him. Later they learned from him that a decade ago, a missionary had come to the same village to share the gospel. The people stoned him to death, but not before one person heard and understood his message—their rescuer.

Although he now trusted Christ, when his faith was fresh and weak many years ago he had fled to the hills in fear for his life. Over time, people grew afraid of him and rumors spread about who he was. Whether he should have come down sooner to share the good news is debatable, but he told his houseguests that when he heard someone was in the village sharing the gospel, he knew he needed to help them or they would face the same fate as the first missionary. The people's fear of him saved the lives of three college students that day. Years later through God working in the lives of just a few, the town became the site of one of the largest churches in the region. God is not afraid of entering dark places. He sees what's ahead.

One evil strategy Satan employs is to sanitize Jesus so much that we imagine He looks away at the nastiest parts of our stories. We might assume He's happy to bless our paths when they are pointing in the right direction, but understand our pain? Sit with us while we face the consequences of our sin? *Never*. However, this couldn't be further from the truth. In fact, anything that begins with the supposition that God expects our perfection is a lie. His very entrance into the world in flesh began with the metaphor that He is comfortable in dark places. He could have been born anytime, to anyone, in any place. He carefully designed an introduction that says in every sense:

- I am coming to you and for you.
- My kingdom is wholly different from anything you've ever seen.
- I am not afraid of entering dirty or dark places.

Anything that begins with the supposition that God expects our perfection is a lie.

Conceived during the Festival of Lights

In Luke 1, we meet Zechariah and Elizabeth, who were the parents of John the Baptist. Zechariah was a priest in the division of Abijah. (There are twelve divisions of priests, and they each have duty one month of the year.) Abijah's priestly duty was in June, and we read in Luke 1:24 that Elizabeth became pregnant shortly after his priestly duty, so perhaps in July. When she was six months pregnant with John the Baptist, she ran into her cousin Mary, the mother of Jesus, who had freshly conceived by the Holy Spirit. In Luke 1:41, we read how John leaped in the womb of his mother at recognizing Mary and Jesus. That would make Mary newly pregnant during Hanukkah. Was the Light of the World conceived during the Festival of Lights?

Born in the Feast of Tabernacles

Assuming Mary carried Jesus nine months, He would have been born in September, which is when Sukkoth falls, the Feast of Tabernacles. In the gospel of John, he wrote in Greek that Jesus "tabernacled" among us. Sukkoth was the one time of the year when shepherds were allowed to bring their animals into the fields to eat whatever hadn't been harvested and to leave a "deposit" of fertilizer for the next planting season. We read in Luke 2:8, "And there were shepherds living out in the fields nearby, keeping watch over their flocks at night."

At night the shepherds kept their flocks in a sheepfold, a natural stone "pen" or a cave. They would use three walls as a barrier and then light a fire in the mouth of the cave, keeping both the animals and the shepherds warm. Imagine what the walls of this cave pen would look like. They would be thick with the soot of a thousand past fires, and the floor would be covered in animal manure. It's time to throw away all the pretty nativity sets we own with clean straw, a plaid blanket, and perfect pine planks. I can't think of a dirtier, nastier place than one with soot, dung, and animals.

Delivered in a dark and dirty place

Then came Mary, pregnant on a donkey, and there was no place for her to give birth. She delivered the Savior of the World in this dirty, dark space. The God of the Story put Himself in the worst chaos because He doesn't just care from afar; He wants to enter our chaos. He has been entering dark and crappy places for a long time. Whatever and wherever we want to invite Him into, He's already there.

The Enemy wants us to believe that some places are so dirty, God won't enter them. He wants us to feel shame and separation from God. However, God isn't afraid of our hard; He isn't shocked or horrified. He is Light, and He came to tabernacle among us. He sent us this message: *There isn't any place, no matter how dark it is, that He won't go.*

One afternoon while I was serving in Haiti, a friend of mine who lived there year-round asked if I would sit in on an English lesson with four gang members who had been coming around his home. They were asking for things he couldn't provide—money, a job, protection—but he was wise enough to know they were circling around actually wanting what they didn't know how to ask for—attention, love, peace. He told them he wanted to get to know them better and suggested some English classes as a means to do so. They agreed, and their first class was on the afternoon I was visiting.

They came into the small classroom where I was already sitting, and immediately I moved onto the floor, essentially sitting at their feet. I had watched enough National Geographic to know that to seem nonthreatening, I should lower my position.

We talked through some vocabulary words. They repeated phrases they had heard from TV and music, and through a translator we clumsily shared a few moments that created a fragile connection.

Finally, it was time for me to leave, and as I stood up, I sensed the Lord prompting me to kiss their foreheads goodbye. It was a ridiculous move and one I silently protested. I had been careful with even making eye contact, but nonetheless, I gently took their faces in my hands and walked down the line, kissing their foreheads with an awkward linger.

The last one physically reacted, looking like I had shocked him. He told our translator he had never had a nonsexual touch from a woman before. I met his eyes and smiled.

I stepped out of the room into the hot Haitian sunshine, not sure why I was there that day, whispering prayers about their future. I'll never forget their faces, and I still pray for their fates.

The next day, I returned home to Cincinnati, feeling very ill. I couldn't get out of bed and was experiencing weird symptoms. By early afternoon, Todd and I were comparing "bulging eyes" and "scaly skin" against an online list of symptoms, checking off the illnesses for which I had been vaccinated.

After an hour of research, Todd looked up. "Beth, do you know what has scaly skin and bulging eyes?" he said slowly. "A snake." Shivering, I closed my eyes, immediately remembering my kiss on the forehead of those boys surrounded in darkness.

"This isn't medical. It's *spiritual*." He confirmed what was dawning on me. Later I received prayer from some friends, and the same afternoon, my symptoms were alleviated.[3]

Diving into chaos will cost us something, but light always wins. When we rub against darkness, it can cling to us, wanting to scare us away. We don't always have the luxury of seeing it hang on us, as I clearly did this day, but when we advance the gospel, we can be assured there is an opposing force.

I've heard it said we can sum up the whole Bible in two words: *come* and *go*. The *come* part is easy—come into His presence, come into the kingdom, come into paradise, come into His arms. The *go* part is more challenging—go into all the world, go make disciples, go and be reconciled with your brother. While *come* brings the deep breath, it's *go* that brings all the scars. We have to lay down our lives on the foundational truth that God will be with us in the going. When we bear scars, when we get hurt or sick, when we're misunderstood or rejected, we share in the suffering of Christ.

As I decide to *go* (have coffee with the friend who is hurting, initiate a conversation with the new neighbor I have no time for, give away what is more comfortable to keep), I am opposed by the one whose agenda is not reconciliation but conflict. Our enemy wants condemnation over redemption and destruction over restoration. I can get halfway into a calling, and chaos will rain down on me. That's when I want to quit. It's easier to protect yourself than to take a risk.

On a radio show I was hosting during the month of October, I posed some questions to the listeners around the topic of Halloween:

- How do you talk to your children about it?
- Do you allow your children to participate in it?
- Do you allow your children to wear costumes of any kind?

Calls ensued with big feelings on both sides, some expressing outrage that Christians would allow a child to participate in pagan rituals, while others saw the holiday as an innocent exercise in fun that they could confidently filter for their children. My cohost and I were moderating the conversation, listening with understanding for both sides, when one caller offered a point of view that changed my thinking on Halloween forever.

"It's my most relationally evangelistic night of the year," he started. "I get a chance to sit on my driveway and look my neighbors in the eye. I can *ooh* and *ahh* over their children, and go above and beyond to serve the adults snacks when kids come up for candy. It's my hope to leave them a positive impression of a Christian I can build on later."

I've never looked at October 31 the same way. I still don't like ghost and witch costumes. I think if people understood the reality of darkness, they wouldn't see it as funny or a form of entertainment. But when I use what might have been intended for evil to instead advance the kingdom of light, it feels redeeming. So now I offer coffee to the adults who come to my porch. I make small talk and try to remember who I engaged with so when Christmas comes, I can offer them each a plate of cookies and take another step toward community engagement. It's become one of my favorite nights of the year, and when I ask questions such as "Which house do you live in?" or "How old is your little Elsa?" I hope they hear curiosity from someone who is interested in who they are.

Instead of avoiding dangerous neighborhoods or shunning gang members or boycotting Halloween, what if we went into those places with our light? We don't have to wonder what our enemy will do; he'll do the same stuff he's always tried to do. We just have to know that stepping into, or forward, is obedience. God will take care of the rest.

How comfortable are you with talking about the supernatural?

Where have you been afraid to go because of darkness?

In which dark place has God tabernacled with you?

Part II

The Scouting Report

"So that we would not be outwitted by Satan; for
we are not ignorant of his designs."
2 Corinthians 2:11 ESV

The following chapters explore Satan's predictable tactics and his intended outcomes for each one:

> *when he'll try to trip us up;*
> *what the collateral damage will be if he wins; and*
> *God's corresponding truth for each one.*

Chapter 6

Satan wants me oblivious.

God wants me vigilant.

"Above all else, guard your heart, for everything you do flows from it."
Proverbs 4:23

This evil one wants us blind to his work in and around our lives. He wins twice when we blame his shenanigans on other people and allow his interference to cause division. He seeps into the world so insidiously, we become comfortable with a certain low level of evil. By the time we ask, "How did this happen?" we have already walked into traps we know better not to. At times I have ignored warning signs because it felt like the path of least resistance, and I have also felt evil work to get a foothold in me until confession was my only way out.

Our daughter Emma was a competitive gymnast for almost nine years. Gymnastics is a world with its own subculture of marathon practices and cut-throat competition. We were living in Mexico at the time, and the higher the level of competition, the tighter the moms bonded. Except for me; I was an outsider. Although I could speak their language, I didn't have the social graces to play that game in my home culture, let alone in a second one. I found it infinitely easier just to manage our interactions, content with being on the outside. I gravitated to another outsider, a beautiful woman who modeled and whose image graced several billboards in town. The other women seemed to be punishing her, so we found each other on the outskirts. We cheered on each other's daughters and sat together during long days of competition.

Emma's practices were typically four hours long, so I took her in the afternoon and Todd picked her up after dinner. One evening, he came home and told me my friend had made him uncomfortable; she was "almost flirting with me," he said.

"No, she wasn't flirting; she's just friendly. There aren't a lot of people who will talk with her." I reassured him, trying to imagine in what universe would she flirt with him. He dropped it until a few nights later when he told me, "Hey, look at this. She bought me a Valentine's Day card. Beth, this is weird."

Again, I laughed it off. "In Spanish, Valentine's Day is called 'the day of friendship and love.' She probably would've given it to whichever one of us had picked Emma up." He tried not to look offended that I was so certain she wasn't interested in him.

My laughing stopped the next week when he came flying through the door, flustered and frustrated, practically yelling how she had followed his car into the parking lot of a local store and communicated in *no uncertain terms* with her words and body what she was hoping would happen—right then while the girls were at practice.

My mind raced to keep up. "What did you do? What did you say?"

He went on to tell me he just got in the car and fled, like Joseph from Potiphar's wife. He called a guy friend on the way and drove straight home.

I closed my eyes, acknowledging what I hadn't before. I felt grief over losing a friend, over not believing Todd, fear, anger, confusion. Bowing my head, I asked God into the space. I didn't trust myself or what I might do or say next. God responded with His peace, affirming my birthright as His daughter, and I looked up at Todd. "I know what I need to do—go and talk with her. Now. Let's go—both of us—and find her …"

He hesitated and looked sideways at me. "Are you sure? Now? What are you going to do? Are you going to *hit her?*"

We both laughed and it broke the building tension. I assured him that wasn't my intention, and we prayed together that God would help us see this night through. We pulled up to the gym, and I saw her right away. My emotions were a combination of anger and sadness. I had a choice in that moment to partner with God or to partner with the Enemy. We live in a war, and even as I marched toward her, I wasn't sure if my sin nature or my Spirit-filled nature would win.

She looked very uncomfortable, eyeing Todd, who stood a step behind me. Looking her in the eyes, I started in about how I knew she was a shiny apple, but what she had to offer Todd was only physical. "And while you have a lot to offer in *that* department, the truth is Todd and I share something more than just physical. It's also spiritual, emotional, relational; it's tied up in history and commitment. God actually has bonded us together …"

She finally lifted her face and met my eyes. She looked so confused.

Dang it. I had come to give her a piece of my mind, and God was putting on full display for me her spiritual depravity, to which I was responsible to respond. "Do you know what I mean by that?"

She shook her head.

I breathed in deeply, hoping I was drawing in some Holy Spirit mixed with the warm Mexican night air. Jesus wanted me to share the gospel with a woman who I could see was partially unclothed under her jacket. God knew all she had tried to do to destroy my marriage, and He was still crazy about her. He wanted her to understand a love she had never experienced, and He was prompting me to testify to it.

So I did.

I won't mischaracterize the story and pretend our friendship bounced right back. I never fully trusted her again, and I own some of that. But it's another example of the Enemy designing an evening of secrecy, shame, lust, and destruction—however, this time he lost.

God won. A husband stood strong, a broken woman heard the gospel, and a wife avoided an assault charge. I am not supposed to look like Jesus only on Sundays and Wednesdays. I am to reflect Him in the heat of any moment when I would prefer to do what I want in my flesh.

Satan subtly takes ideas that are true, God ideas, and twists them. It's why they are easy to swallow; they *seem* right. When I align to what isn't true, brokenness ensues (sometimes I am broken, sometimes I break others). Truth builds, lies break. A lie might cause me to run into a wall, or run out of steam, or run in circles, but living a life based on half-truths eventually causes destruction. Though defeated at the cross, Satan is still dangerous (John 8:44; 10:10; 1 Pet. 5:8), but we have the power to resist him and his influence in our lives (1 Pet. 5:9; James 4:7). In this war between good and evil, I can be tempted to think people are my source of struggle, when in reality, spiritual powers in the heavenly realm (Eph. 6:12) are the source. When I focus on people alone, sides are taken between "us" and "them," and I dangerously see myself as something to be propped up or defended. When I see what's truly going on around me with spiritual glasses on, I am far more willing to respond supernaturally.

Often what the Enemy starts can be turned on him. Paul was a biblical master at this:

- Put me in jail, and I'll share the gospel with the jailer.
- Give me a thorn in the flesh, and I'll testify to God's faithfulness.
- Put me on trial, and I'll take the opportunity to shout God's truth to a crowd.

We have to be sensitive to how much of the world we are swallowing, enough to be conversant with others, but not so much that we get used to the taste of it. Without realizing it, we consume the Enemy's kingdom through a steady diet of media, literature, and the arts, all the while working up an appetite for his way. We can erroneously believe all evil is dripping in black paint and bloodstains, obvious from the moment we see it. But lots of evil sounds and looks loving and light. The Enemy is a deceiver and wants us unaware of what we are into until it's too late.

> We have to be sensitive to how much of the world we are swallowing, enough to be conversant with others, but not so much that we get used to the taste of it.

What is wrong can feel so natural that, in my confusion, I can advance the wrong agenda. I might say something seemingly loving but unbiblical. I tolerate bite-sized sin, not realizing I am compromising. I might think a little bit of deception, profanity, selfishness, or judgment is fine because it makes me interesting or relatable. I am trying to open my eyes and not be ignorant to his slithering-snake-in-my-garden ways.

Some people today wave their unanswered questions as flags of honor in the name of authenticity. They prefer to "be real" and broadcast their doubts rather than press in and cry to Jesus, like the man in Mark 9:24, "I believe; help my unbelief" (ESV). These outspoken believers dishonor God in an attempt to be "relatable." We have to first give God credit and admit we can't do anything on our own.

I am concerned about messages going out from the Church that say our futures are *ours* to determine, our abilities are only limited by our belief in *ourselves*. I don't believe in myself; I am, quite frankly, hot and cold on the same day, victorious and fractured practically in the same breath. I know I am loved by God, forgiven for my sin, sanctified in all ways, but I am still a walking-around-most-days mess. I believe in what God says about me, but it's *through Him* that all things are possible. While I do think we need to pursue an authentic faith, I want to make sure my doubts aren't seeping through a foundation of faith and destroying what God has worked within me to build.

When considering vigilance, I think about having my guard up with an enemy who is dark and evil. However, I also need a strategy to vet ideas that come from good places, with good intentions, but that feed me unbiblical ideas I like to hear. Plenty of people want to tell me my life is what I make of it, and it is in my hands, and the world is waiting for me to be my best self. But the gospel says:

> Then Jesus told his disciples, "If anyone would come after me, let him deny himself and take up his cross and follow me. For whoever would save his life will lose it, but whoever loses his life for my sake will find it. For what will it profit a man if he gains the whole world and forfeits his soul? Or what shall a man give in return for his soul?" (Matt. 16:24–26 ESV)

I strengthen my foundation of faith by spending time with God and reading His Word.

Where are you more aware of the Enemy's schemes?

Where are you involved in compromise right now? What can you do about it?

How has the Enemy infiltrated your entertainment choices?

Chapter 7

Satan wants me proud.

God guides me to humility.

"These are the ones I look on with favor: those who are humble
and contrite in spirit, and who tremble at my word."
Isaiah 66:2

Orphan Sunday is like Super Bowl weekend to someone in my field. Every year our team receives numerous requests from churches who would like a speaker, and together we weigh the options. One year, while I had a place I was leaning toward, the others thought I should go to a church who had invested significantly in our ministry and where we hadn't been invited before. I agreed, and leading up to the weekend, I collaborated with the church's creative team about the message I would deliver. However, I was hyper-aware—since they mentioned it a dozen times—that I would be their first female speaker on a weekend. I tried to downplay it; my plan was to show up, tell impactful stories of orphaned children, and pray that God would be glorified.

I set out on my six-hour drive to arrive for their Saturday-evening service. On the way there, I practiced my message to my windshield several times and felt good about it. But I immediately knew something was wrong when the pastor didn't meet me in the lobby as planned and instead sent a staff member.

"Beth, I don't know how to say this," he started, apologetically. "Our leadership has had a change of heart. We just don't feel comfortable with a woman sharing the main message. Our pastor will be delivering the sermon, and we've allotted three minutes for you to share a 'minute for ministry.' Please share your heart about orphans, and we'll make a big deal about people coming to see you at your table."

I smiled, because I have people skills, but inside I was angry. *I could have been somewhere else this weekend. You should have thought about this before now. I am better than you are giving me credit for. I am better than you!* It only took a second to trigger my pride, and I am sad to report, I never really recovered before I took the stage. As I sat through worship, I stewed, *If I only get three minutes, it will be the best three minutes you have ever seen. In fact, I'll make my three minutes better than your thirty!* Despite my earlier prayers, my sin of pride blocked the Spirit's movement and I fumbled my way terribly through those three minutes. I knew *as it was happening* that the congregation must silently be thinking, *Glad we don't have to sit through another twenty-seven minutes of this!*

After the service, I stumbled out of the auditorium (forget the table in the lobby!) and found a back hallway. I was some combination of mad and embarrassed, and I knew I needed Jesus. Closing myself off in a dark classroom, I sunk to the floor. While praying, I felt a nudge to call a man named Dave, the first pastor to invite me to share a Sunday-morning message with a large congregation. I hadn't talked to him in years and wasn't sure why I was being prompted to call *him*. I wanted to call my mother, who would tell me I was amazing, or my husband, who would defend me. Why would God want me to call Dave?

I found his number in my contacts and hoped it was still the same. "Dave?" I started in as soon as he answered, but I could hear the tears threatening in my voice. "Hi, it's Beth Guckenberger." I sensed his surprise to hear from me, and I could hear a crowd in the background.

I quickly plowed on, "I am out of town this weekend at a church, and they won't let me share my stories on their stage, and I pridefully tried to show off tonight, and I blew it, and now I am frustrated, and I was praying, and I felt prompted to call …" I was just one long run-on sentence. "I wanted to say thank you for all those years ago, you allowing me to share at your church. You helped build in me a healthy confidence to take a stage and share the truth. I blew it tonight, but there's still tomorrow, right? I just wanted to say thank you for believing in me …"

He took a deep breath, and I could almost hear him smile. He had been a pastor for thirty years, and I knew I was about to be shepherded. "Beth, tonight I am speaking to college students and I was just wondering to myself if I still had it—that ability to call dreams out in others. Your call right now is God's affirmation He heard my wondering. Thank you for calling. Now go spend enough time with God tonight that tomorrow morning when you go back up there, you speak to Him and not the church."

We hung up, and I let my head fall back against the wall. When I find myself mired in pride and facing the earthly consequences, will I always remember to call out to God? *I hope so.* In the span of a few minutes, He had encouraged me, He had encouraged Dave, and He had released me from a spirit of performance that allowed me to effectively share from my heart the next day.

Years later, I had the opportunity to speak at an adoption and foster retreat. Afterward, a woman approached me with a picture. "You don't know me," she started, "but I attend a church where you shared years ago on Orphan Sunday." I smiled and waited for her to continue. "At the time, my husband and I were having the on-again-off-again conversation about adopting. We were on different pages, but something you said that morning pushed us together and we began the process of adoption." She showed me a Christmas picture of her large, multi-racial family, all eight children in matching pajamas. "Thank you for coming and sharing your heart and story with us. Our family will be forever changed."

I never get tired of hearing how God places children in families. I smiled warmly and asked, "Thank you for sharing this with me. Where do you go to church?" I was thinking through some of the great opportunities I'd had over the years.

When she mentioned the congregation I spoke to for only three minutes, I laughed out loud. Of course, Jesus! I could feel the emotion building in me as I held her picture—both tenderness toward God for allowing me to hear this testimony and conviction that my pride counted differently than God did that day. He wasn't looking at the clock, or how many people were there. He saw only a family on the brink of their calling. He needed a vessel to bring His testimony. He could do what He wanted in ten seconds, let alone three minutes.

I went that weekend for them, for me, for Dave, for probably a million reasons I still don't know. I did not go there to be impressive, or to be a tradition breaker, or to prove anything. I am called to be obedient. God simply counts differently than we do, which makes pride in our things and our accomplishments foolish.

God simply counts differently than we do, which makes pride in our things and our accomplishments foolish.

God desires humility in people. Throughout Scripture, He points it out and rewards it. When we are prideful and focused on our own achievement, it gets between Him and us. It's exactly why our enemy loves our ego so much; it's a natural divider. Our spiritual health depends on relying on God.

I need Him for salvation, direction, and indwelling of the gifts. Pride grows when I falsely believe my achievements, gifts, or resources are because of me and, as a result, that I deserve them.

Satan had it all—intelligence, beauty, and power—but his sin of pride caused him to believe those gifts were of his doing and gave him special rights. In the Garden of Eden, Satan whispered to Adam and Eve, "You will be as God." This is what pride does; it tries to elevate us to the level of God, as if what we have been given makes us like Him. It is a dangerous way to think, and why the Devil loves it. When we are certain our way is best, we don't confess sin, we don't ask God for direction, and we aren't humble in front of others. And the collateral damage is poor testimony, earthly consequences to our shortsighted decisions, and separation from God. Pride goes before the fall (Prov. 16:18), and being aware of this evil tactic can prevent disastrous consequences to decisions we try to make all on our own.

Yes, the Enemy stirred up fear in the leadership of the church, pride in me, struggle within a marriage, and self-doubt in a retired pastor …

But he overplayed his hand, and God won. *Every time.*

In what area of your life do you struggle with pride? What can you do about it?

When has God taught you a lesson about pride?

Where do you struggle not to count from a worldly perspective?

Chapter 8

Satan wants me isolated.

God made me for community.

"Joab said, 'If the Arameans are too strong for me, then you are to rescue me; but if the Ammonites are too strong for you, then I will rescue you. Be strong, and let us fight bravely for our people and the cities of our God.'"
1 Chronicles 19:12-13

It was 2007, and I pulled into the ministry campus in Mexico where I was working, driving a new Honda Odyssey minivan. In the front seat sat a life-long friend of Todd's and mine, a mentor who was in the country visiting us. As we were climbing out of the car, a guest walked up and said sarcastically, "When I grow up, I want to be a missionary, so *I* can drive a new car."

I started to open my mouth and tell him where the car had come from, but our friend put his hand on my arm and said quietly, "You don't owe him an explanation; just tell him something you know for sure is true."

Startled, I blurted out before I could think, "Jesus is the giver of all good gifts." I was quoting the book of James, but I didn't say that. The man had already turned away after delivering his message. I faced my friend, who was one step ahead of me and drawing something on the carry-out napkin he held in his hand.

"Beth, look at this. It's a house with a front porch, a yard, and a neighbor-hood. All your relationships fall into one of these four communities. People are either in your home, on your metaphorical front porch, in your yard, or out there somewhere in your neighborhood. Where did that man fall?"

"In my neighborhood," I replied, not even sure of his name.

"If someone in your house wants to know where the car came from, share it. It's a testimony your household can grow from knowing." I nodded, following him to a bench.

He turned to me. "If someone on your front porch asks where the car came from, it might be with the intention of accountability or to share an answered prayer, but regardless, you've put them in an important place in your life. Tell them the story of your van! But if someone in your yard or neighborhood wants to know, it needs to be because you want to share, not because they've asked. You don't owe them any explanation."

As I've talked to people in our age of oversharing, I've probably now drawn that same little house on a hundred napkins. It's been a tool in my tool belt to teach both about discretion and about the importance of valuing our front-porch-life witnesses. We have an enemy who wants us to feel like everyone is the same—all at an arm's length. It would be to his delight if we were to feel as though no one really *knew* us. Regardless of how many "friends" we have on social media, or contacts in our phone, he wants us to feel alone. If he can isolate us, then we can't share our lives, we can't ask for help, and we can't collaborate and work together. Isolation is as old as the Garden of Eden, and although today the attacks are more sophisticated, we live in a world full of lonely people.

When my twelve-year-old son, Tyler, was newly adopted into our family, the first week in his American junior high, his class was assigned a heritage project. The students were tasked with creating poster-board displays to introduce themselves and tell about their childhood. But because we had adopted Tyler from a Mexican government children's home, we didn't have much information, let alone pictures, from his childhood. He was in a total panic at the thought of divulging his history to these strangers.

I took out my pen and drew that familiar little house. "Your classmates are currently in your yard. I hope one day they come onto your porch and you can share where you've been and how God found us and put us together as a family. But for now, they are in your yard and we don't owe them anything." I looked at him, making sure he was following. "We are going to google 'cute Hispanic baby' and pick one to print on picture paper." He giggled, amazed I was allowing such deception. I went on, "We won't frame any of those pictures for Grandma; she's on our front porch. But for your class, we can keep them where they are until they have earned your trust."

He understood what I meant, and we finished his project to the satisfaction of his grade and the class's curiosity. The Enemy *loves* when we overshare and put information out to the world that can be used against us. Ironically, it can make us feel more isolated when we overshare. Like an admission that I don't have a friend to tell this to—so, world, here it is.

Is there a place for vulnerability, to be our authentic selves and have truths reinforced until trust is built? Yes! When I invest in my home and connect with those on my front porch, it reminds me of biblical truths like God is with me or God uses people to demonstrate His practical care for me. From those connections, I can offer overflowing strength to those in my yard and neighborhood.

The problem is that with increased use of social media, we've lost all discernment. We've opened the gates and doors and windows, and now strangers know what the insides of our houses look like. They've heard our intimate confessions online, and it's cultivated a false sense of intimacy. Knowing about me isn't the same as being known. If I keep filling my dance card with people who "like" me or "friend" me but don't exchange real fears, ideas, and experiences, I stay isolated. Seen but not known. Exposed and not safe.

Knowing about me isn't the same as being known.

With increasing disconnection, maybe for reasons that have nothing to do with each other, over time I can feel touchy, almost sensitive, or even worse, insensitive. This leads to judgment, hiding, less vulnerability, and before I know it, I isolate because it feels better to count on myself rather than my brothers and sisters. Isolation leads to all the words that start with *self*: self-absorbed, self-centered, self-conscious, self-contempt, self-destructive, self-justification, self-pity, self-righteous. When I fall into those traps, I am ripe for an enemy attack.

I need people in my life whom I trust to watch my back, and those kinds of relationships require investment, not mere management. When I form a connection with someone, it necessitates nurturing, and a spiritual bond all the more so. The Enemy will purposefully use my weakness and work to disconnect us.

There's a passage in 1 Chronicles about two brothers who see enemies coming on multiple fronts and vow to have each other's backs:

> Joab saw that there were battle lines in front of him and behind him; so he selected some of the best troops in Israel and deployed them against the Arameans. He put the rest of the men under the command of Abishai his brother, and they were deployed against the Ammonites. Joab said, "If the Arameans are too strong for me, then you are to rescue me; but if the Ammonites are too strong for you, then I will rescue you. Be strong, and let us fight bravely for our people and the cities of our God. The LORD will do what is good in his sight." (19:10–13)

In Genesis 4, God was talking to Cain, the brother of Abel. Cain was the bad one (where we get the expression "raising Cain") who eventually murdered his brother. God warned him in verse 7, "You will be accepted if you do what is right. But if you refuse to do what is right, then watch out! Sin is crouching at the door, eager to control you. But you must subdue it and be its master" (NLT).

We have to be self-aware of the sins crouching at our doors. They're different for each of us—a combination of childhood experiences, generational patterns, bad habits, personality weaknesses, and trauma. Satan knows exactly what's at my door, and he knocks repeatedly, hoping temptation will cause me to open it. Though when I do open it, and sin masters me in the moment, there will always be grace. The Bible promises no condemnation, but earthly consequences will ensue, and the sin I show the Enemy, he will use readily against me.

The shame I feel when I see my sin at the door, and it defeats me, drives me to isolation. It's where we start to think things like *If they really knew what I am/do/think ... or If I can protect this (whatever this is), then I am safe.* Isolation is fertile ground for distorted thinking. It allows lies to linger. The Enemy has used this trick since David and Peter—people who fell to sin and needed their communities for restoration. God doesn't get stuck in the day we are experiencing isolation and feeling out of fighting shape. He sees what's coming and is cheering us on to get up, look up, and keep punching. Not sinning isn't an option; we are fallen. Allowing sin to create space between us and our people? That's allowing the Enemy to use the same bullet twice on us, and in this war, we can't afford it.

Who is on your front porch?

Where are you dangerously isolated? What can you do about it?

What sins are crouching at your door?

Chapter 9

Satan wants me selfish.

God made me to serve.

"But if you harbor bitter envy and selfish ambition in your hearts, do not boast about it or deny the truth. Such 'wisdom' does not come down from heaven but is earthly, unspiritual, demonic. For where you have envy and selfish ambition, there you find disorder and every evil practice."
Jomes 3:14-16

Our adversary wants us to be obsessed with self. When we are, we don't see others or their needs. We don't see God's creation or His work around us. Nothing points to a supernatural God faster than someone sacrificing for the needs of another.

In early 2020, Todd and I had the amazing opportunity to travel to Davos, Switzerland, for the World Economic Forum. We knew fancy people from all over the world would attend, exchanging fancy ideas in fancy clothes, and going was admittedly an intimidating idea. We believed in what we were there to present—trauma training for frontline workers who invest in the lives of vulnerable children—but while there, we would be meeting astronauts and environmental entrepreneurs. On its own, the company was daunting; but in addition, most conversations were relatively competitive with lots of passing around of business cards. You learned quickly to advocate for yourself if you were going to be heard.

While exciting in many regards, we honestly felt out of place. Our training and preference were to be curious about others and ask good questions, but the system seemed to punish those who didn't self-promote. We were doing the best we could, but it felt uncomfortable at times.

One afternoon, we took a break from networking to walk around Davos as tourists. We checked out the exhibits and asked each other, "Why are we here?" While in the Johnson & Johnson display, we struck up a conversation with one of the staff, but after telling her what we did, we realized we had very little common ground with her. As we turned to leave, she muttered something about wishing we were in health care. She had a cancellation for a panel in thirty minutes and needed someone who could speak about the intersection of health care and innovation.

Todd and I looked at each other. One of the people in our delegation was the CEO of a company that was using new software to identify diabetes in third-world countries and to treat eye complications. He would be perfect, but who knew where he was at that moment? We decided to divide and conquer: Todd ran in his business suit almost thirty minutes to where we had last seen him, working his WhatsApp to find him. I stayed and advocated for him to be their panelist (even though I had *just* met him). It worked! Our new friend ran back with Todd and had a great opportunity to share his vision and product to an audience who received him well.

That evening found us at yet another dinner with people in small conversations talking about their "thing," but there was also some buzz about us—how we had inconvenienced ourselves and taken time to further someone else's cause. In the end, we actually got more exposure and respect out of doing things God's way than if we had talked about ourselves and continued to push our own agenda.

Late that night, lying in the dark, we reflected on how that day we felt more comfortable than any of the previous ones: in part because doing things God's way just *feels* better afterward. For all the work we do to posture ourselves up front, it's actually more impressive and satisfying to be selfless.

I tend to struggle most with being selfish when I am hurting—either physically, emotionally, or relationally. My natural instinct is to self-protect and use defensive strategies like manipulation, aggression, triangulation, and control. They come from the strong need to take care of me at the expense of you. It's one of the reasons the Enemy feasts on our painful situations. He knows we are vulnerable to further sin.

I tend to struggle most with being selfish when I am hurting.

C. S. Lewis wrote:

> If I am confessing my sin (I snapped, I was impatient, I was short …) I immediately think to myself I was provoked. I want to let myself off the hook. It popped out before I could stop it, or in other words, that is what is truly in my heart before I had time to disguise it. If there are rats in a cellar, you are most likely to see them if you go in very suddenly. But the suddenness does not create the rats; it only prevents them from hiding. In the same way, the suddenness of the provocation does not make me an ill-tempered man: it only shows me what an ill-tempered man I am. The rats are always there in the cellar, but if you go in shouting and noisily, they will have taken cover before you switch on the light.[4]

I have to be honest: there are some rats in my cellar, and most of the time I can put my best foot forward and no one sees them; but I know that when I am in pain or feel provoked, my selfish tendencies often emerge. I have been trying to reverse engineer my thinking and ask myself how the Enemy could use my selfish feelings to tempt me toward self-destructive behaviors. I am weak in times of extreme fatigue, physical pain, and emotional desperation, and I know my next decisions can be toward self-interest (and bring costly consequences) or they can be about sacrifice (and bring tremendous blessing).

The fruit of selfishness is frustration, because nothing is ever enough to satisfy outside of Christ. There will always be circumstances I do not like and cannot control, and if I don't learn to adapt and serve, I will naturally default to aggression, whether passive or overt. When I feel dysregulated, I ask myself, *How did I get here? How did I try to meet my own needs, and was it at the expense of someone else?*

James 3:14–16 teaches us:

> But if you harbor bitter envy and selfish ambition in your hearts, do not boast about it or deny the truth. Such "wisdom" does not come down from heaven but is earthly, unspiritual, demonic. For where you have envy and selfish ambition, there you find disorder and every evil practice.

James 3 says that selfishness and envy are demonic. They result in disorder, and chaos is the very goal of our enemy. It may sound good, or look pretty, or come out of a smiling mouth, but it's no less demonic. The Devil has set the table, and now the main course is exactly what *he's* been cooking up. In contrast, God brings His peace into disorder. He modeled that with total sacrifice.

The Enemy can't force me to be demanding or egotistical; I do that just fine on my own. I have certain limitations, and if I don't ask God for more of Him to compensate for the weakness in me, then I am triggered, sin results, and the Devil wins. As I reach my limitation, my nature itches to satisfy itself (*give in*), and I have choices: Will I confess my thinking? Will I run to God for spiritual rest? If I don't go to God for rest, inevitably selfishness will manifest as impatience, intolerance, neediness, greediness, and pride. The result is a focus on me, my needs, and myself.

All that *me*-focus hurts the relationships in my life. Whether things crash in a conflict, leaving me feeling caught in my sin and forced to apologize or defend, or in an internal conviction, I need God to be my Healer.

At this point I have to identify the differences between:

> *Guilt*: something I feel because I've done something bad and don't know what to do about it.
> *Shame*: something I feel because I (believe I) am bad.
> And *conviction*: the prompting of the Holy Spirit to confess my sins. Conviction brings freedom because I realize in His image and by His sacrifice, I am made right in His eyes.

When I feel convicted about my selfishness, now God can mature me. The most selfish humans in the world are infants; they have needs they demand are met. As we grow physically, so does the expectation that we will develop out of that selfishness. I don't have to demand my needs be met; I can be in relationship with my heavenly Father and ask for what I need from Him. When I hear myself being selfish, I realize I am acting like an infant.

Besides walking in the Spirit, what can I do about my selfishness? Develop healthy relationships that create better self-awareness. The good words and experiences deposited in my life inform my sense of self. Although those are best deposited in us as children, any relationship can be improved through listening and play, good words, and experiences.

Those meaningful relationships are like kryptonite to my selfishness. They give me motivation to be unselfish as I am learning to love well the people in my life.

When do you struggle most with being selfish? What can you do about it?

What rats are in your cellar?

What role have you seen confession play with selfishness?

Chapter 10

Satan wants me discouraged.

God emboldens me.

"The wicked flee though no one pursues, but
the righteous are as bold as a lion."
Proverbs 28:1

For Back2Back's twentieth anniversary, we invited anyone who had been
involved over the last two decades to come to an open house. All night long, I
reconnected with old friends and met new people who shared how their lives
had been impacted by mission trips or through child sponsorship.

A young woman approached me and asked shyly, "Do you remember
me?" I searched her face but didn't recognize her. She continued, "I was
thirteen when I first went to Mexico, and you taught one night on James
1:27 and how true religion is to take care of widows and orphans in their
distress …" I nodded for her to keep going—that *sounded* like me.

She said, "I made a commitment in my heart during the trip that I was
going to grow up and serve orphans—*somehow*. Well, it's been fifteen years,
and now my husband and I"—she opened her coat to reveal an impossibly
small infant in a baby carrier—"we foster medically fragile children in our
county. I just wanted you to know." I was stunned and overwhelmed. I don't
remember my exact response to her, but her story was so moving to me that
I retold it multiple times the remainder of the evening.

A year later, we met again at a conference where I was speaking, and I asked her how she was doing since I saw her last.

She smiled. "Actually, we still have the little girl you met that night." She then pulled out her phone to show me a recent picture. "We have spent most of this year preparing for her adoption."

I beamed back at her. "Congratulations! That's great news."

Her smile fell some. "Actually, her birth mother has made some changes in her life, and now the county has a reunification plan in place. Next month, we'll be returning her."

I reached out and touched her arm. "How are you doing?" Although wonderful the child would return to her birth mother, she would be losing the only mother she had known. It was a complicated adoption situation, and I wanted to acknowledge there are always big feelings when this happens.

She smiled anew. "At first I was really frustrated. I thought I had heard from God to pursue the adoption, and now He was taking her away. I thought the *baby* was my mission, and now without her, I would be without a mission ..." She looked up at me to see if I was following. I had walked in her shoes and was for sure tracking with her.

She continued, "Then eventually, I took my pain and questions to the Lord. He gently reminded me that the way I feel about the baby is how He feels about her mother. And if He lives in me, then I could feel this kind of love for her too." I saw in her face what this lesson had cost her. "I started praying for the mom, eventually texting her pictures of her daughter. Slowly, over the last couple of months, we have formed a friendship. She's asked me if I would be her daughter's godmother. So I guess we'll stay connected now forever."

I shook my head and thought immediately about John 3:16, "God so loved the world ..." He is such a good "so-lover." He *so loved* this woman in our county that sixteen years ago, He planted a seed in a teenage girl. He made sure it was watered so at this moment, when that mother most needed to understand how God sees her and feels about her, He would have this living representation of Him reaching out to her, with *hope*.

Satan wanted a baby separated from her mother, he wanted a foster mom despairing and disillusioned, and he wanted the birth mother to feel alone and ashamed. Instead, we have a Jesus follower pursuing someone outside of God's family, we have a baby with double the support, and we have a birth mom receiving messages of grace, mercy, and love. Adversary *defeated*.

As Christ followers, we are to put God on display, and when we do, no matter what Satan intends, God will use it for good. Will it get messy and hard? Yes, of course, coming close to pain is expensive; it will cost us something. Disappointment may cause me to want to give up along the way, thinking it will never happen. But when we participate in God's story, and we identify with His sacrifice, we gain what we can never lose. Encouragement keeps me in fighting shape with hope and the perspective that the fight is always worth it!

Hope is the birthmark of God's kids. God asked His family to hope for a Promised Land, to hope for a Savior, to hope for His return. Hope is more than wishful thinking; it's spiritual confidence God will always provide. Hope makes us bold, and the Enemy prefers us downcast and timid. As the opposite of hope, discouragement is subtle but sticky. Once it seeps in, it can be hard to shake off.

When we are down, sometimes people falsely think we need to be "cheered up." But what we need is to be reminded where our perspective comes from. A friend and I were planning a retreat, and she was dejected that some people were bowing out and the details were not coming together easily. It wouldn't work to distract her or be fake with "It'll all be fine" or, worse yet, "You shouldn't feel that way." Instead, I reminded her of what's true: God will do what He wants with our plans and He is to be trusted. This simultaneously helped me, because discouragement can be infectious.

Proverbs 28:1 says, "The wicked flee though no one pursues, but the righteous are as bold as a lion." Whether it's because I am getting older or just nervier, I speak my mind more than I used to. I feel frustrated by a culture that allows injustice and a spiritual enemy to delight in our personal downfalls. I can't be a lion concerned about the whole jungle, but in my own corner, I am feeling bold. Winston Churchill once said, "I was not the lion, but it fell to me to give the lion's roar." Whether we always feel like it or not, it's time to speak truth, be a light, and fight. Discouragement thrives in inactivity and won't get traction when we're in motion.

I want to walk into rooms that are easier to avoid, because I *believe* I can represent God's family and heart. I want to speak up when it's easier just to go along, because "good intentions" aren't enough; I need to take a stand and lead others. I want to take more risks, knowing even if something doesn't turn out how I hoped, there are still lessons in it for me. I want to value that growth over other measures of success. Lions aren't subtle, so no more thinking I have to be underwhelming or unintimidating. That's just discouragement and intimidation speaking. As a wife, mother, friend, worker, leader, I hope I am both tenderly fierce and thoughtfully courageous.

As a wife, mother, friend, worker, leader, I hope I am both tenderly fierce and thoughtfully courageous.

Discouragement keeps me focused on self-protection, but God has allowed me, like a bold lion, to exercise His protection over those I love. God is my first Protector, and when I act in this way, I hope to be modeling His nature in me. I want to protect my family, the Bible, the defenseless. I want to protect vulnerable children and the freedoms I currently enjoy. Lions are bold and willing to fight, so I hope never to back down from the opportunity to defend God or those He's entrusted into my care. Everyone in the jungle knows where they stand with a lion, and the lion's confidence is unmistakable. May that be said of us.

When is a time you've held on to God's truth in the middle of a confusing season?

Where do you find yourself easily discouraged? What can you do about it?

What would you do if you were bolder?

Chapter 11

Satan wants me afraid.

God makes me brave.

"Be strong and courageous. Do not be afraid; do not be discouraged,
for the Lord your God will be with you wherever you go."
Joshua 1:9

I received a text from an unknown number: "Tyler forgot his soccer shoes,
can you bring them to school?"

Our newly adopted son didn't have a cell phone, so I assumed it had
come from one of his friends. Tyler was in seventh grade, having joined our
family a few months prior. It was game day, so I left work and went home
to investigate. Sure enough, his soccer bag rested by the door, left in the
morning rush. I grabbed it and headed to the school. After I arrived, I rushed
inside the building, then found him in an athlete study hall.

"Forget something?" I asked, smiling, as I approached his table.

His face lit up. "It worked!" he marveled. "I told my teammates I couldn't
play because I didn't remember to bring my cleats. They told me my mom
would bring them to school. I didn't know moms did that. But look! You're
here!" He forgot where he was for a moment and threw his arms around me.

Hugging him back, I murmured something in his ear about how moms
do this kind of thing *all* the time. I realized his understanding of the parent-
child relationship was brand-new. Having spent most of his childhood in a

government orphanage, he didn't understand all the rights that came with being someone's child. I was getting a chance to show him how it worked.

John 1:12 says, "To all who did receive him, to those who believed in his name, he gave the right to become children of God." As God's kid, I have rights I don't fully appreciate and definitely don't always take advantage of. One of those rights is never to be afraid. Fear drives all kinds of behavior in me. It can cause me to spin in circles, pull back, and feel frozen. The Enemy messes with the atmosphere, pushes on my weaknesses, and as a result, I worry or feel anxious. It's as crazy as Tyler not playing in his game, when I was more than willing to bring him his shoes. God is more than willing to offer me peace, and yet sometimes I sit out, forgetting my rights as His kid.

God says some 365 times in our Bibles: *"Fear not."* He's not oblivious to the circumstances we find ourselves in. We can be lost, physically hurt, in a war, or brokenhearted, but since God works with us from the inside, regardless of our context, we can experience His *shalom*.

Shalom is the Hebrew word meaning "peace" and is defined as "complete, wholeness, a literal filling in of our cracks." When we don't ask God to fill in those cracks, what's exposed is vulnerable to the Enemy. If we are afraid or worried, that enemy can literally *steal* our time as we envision over and over all the possibilities.

Here is where we can see the Enemy overplay his hand. He very predictably frightens us (about our past, our present, politics, our health, the economy, our relationships, *anything*!), and while we sit in fear, we move further away from God. If I can see this coming, before the emotion hits me too hard, I can recognize its source as evil and use that to galvanize my conviction to stand strong instead of succumb to anxiety.

I try to practice this every day. If a child is late, instead of worrying he or she has been in a car accident, I just say, "Not today, Satan. I will not give you one ounce of my thought life." Then I use this moment to pray for my kid's life and future. If someone I love gets a diagnosis I don't like, instead of being afraid for a future *that hasn't been written yet*, I say, "God, I'm so grateful You use all things and will be glorified in this story. Involve me in what You are doing."

Satan has gotten ridiculous mileage out of this simple trick of causing fear. He wanted Moses afraid of Pharaoh and Elijah afraid of Baal. He tried to scare godly women like Mary, Esther, and Hannah. He even attempted to frighten Jesus in the wilderness. But if I can see fear not as my weakness but as Satan's trickery, I am quicker to denounce it and move on in God's strength. When I forget to do that, though, anger usually ensues. Fear is a primary emotion, and lots of destruction sits on top of it.

> If I can see fear not as my weakness but as Satan's trickery, I am quicker to denounce it and move on in God's strength.

Todd and I built a house, which was mostly a fun process. We picked out carpet and lighting features and dreamed about a home that would fit our unusually large family. One night I came home and he was looking at pictures of bathroom features. I was confused.

"Do you want to change something we ordered?" I asked, starting off innocently.

"I am thinking we need to add a bathroom to the guest room," he stated.

"Why?" I challenged, feeling immediately feisty. "We have plenty of bathrooms."

"I think our guests, especially the long-term ones, will like having privacy," he countered.

And we were off. We started talking about bathrooms, but before long we were arguing about his mother and past conflicts, and I was angry. We had just learned in a trauma training at work that anger, in all its forms, is a secondary emotion. When we are angry, we are actually afraid.[5] I wasn't thinking about that training, though; I was thinking about winning the argument with Todd that we didn't need a bathroom in the guest room.

He, however, had more composure at the moment and reminded me of the teaching. "Beth, you seem angry. What are you afraid of?"

I paused longer than I would like to admit. Taking a deep breath, I confessed, "I am afraid we can't afford it."

He slid some papers in front of me and pointed to a column. "Look at my calculations. We can definitely afford it, or I wouldn't have brought it up."

Once my concerns were relieved, the anger dissipated. "Okay," I said and smiled, "then I'd like brushed nickel."

If the Enemy can keep us afraid, we will sit in our anger. Sometimes my anger is loud and abrasive, causing obvious collateral damage, and sometimes my anger is quiet and passive, creating distance between me and whoever feels threatening. Either way, fear is one of the Enemy's best tools to destroy relationship and opportunity.

If I can't articulate my fears, let alone ask God to fight them with me, the Enemy has me right where he wants me. I become angry, and that reaction manifests itself in places that might not have anything to do with my original fear. I can be afraid of my health or finances and take it out on my child or while driving. I can be afraid that I am not enough, or that something isn't going to change, and my quiet anger manifests in rage. The answer is remembering I am God's kid, a child of God, and with this identity, I have the right to never be afraid again.

What privileges come with being one of God's kids?

When have you felt Him fill in your cracks?

What scares you? What can you do about it?

Chapter 12

Satan wants me to feel lost.

God never loses sight of me.

"Give careful thought to the paths for your feet and be steadfast in all your ways. Do not turn to the right or the left; keep your foot from evil."
Proverbs 4:26-27

Being lost is a helpless feeling. One time I was driving in London with a friend, on what felt like the wrong side of the road, trying to get to a town ninety minutes out of the city center. After countless roundabouts and hours of frustration, I stopped for the fifth time to ask at a gas station how to get onto the highway system. Someone heard my accent and, sensing my brimming tears, offered to lead us through a tricky part of traffic until we were on the right route. I couldn't have done that on my own; I needed leading.

In the same way, when we get spiritually lost and are spinning in circles on what feels like the wrong side of the road, we need help navigating tricky paths. One of the Enemy's greatest tools is disorientation. He wants me to feel so turned around I couldn't ever make my way back home. This is where I require a Savior, because as much as I'd like to say *yes* to that proverb "keep your foot from evil," my foot has found itself more than once stepping in the wrong direction.

Bible teacher Ray Vander Laan was the first person to introduce me to the Hebrew word *go'el*.[6] In English it means "redeem," which sounds like a very Jesus word, but it's actually a patriarchal term coming from an ancient culture familiar to God's Old Testament family.

In that era, imagine "Tom" is the patriarch of a family. All his siblings, their spouses and children, everything belonging to them is Tom's, but he is responsible to care for the entire family with those resources. If someone in the family is lost (captured by an enemy, or hurt and gone), the job of father Tom is to pay whatever ransom or price necessary to bring them back into the household. Even if someone loses a piece of property, or sells it when he or she shouldn't have, it's the father's job to use his resources to get the piece back. Redemption means bringing what is lost back to the father's house, whatever the cost.

When God tells His people He will redeem them, He is saying, *I will go and find you, use My resources, and bring you back to the Father's house.* He says He can redeem us from our enemies (Ps. 135), He can redeem us from a life in the pit (Ps. 103), and He can redeem us from trouble (Ps. 107). What does our adversary want? He wants us in the pit and in trouble. He wants to block the redemptive work of God in our lives, because the last thing he desires is our restoration to the Father's house.

Biblically, God is the Father; He's our patriarch. He gave all His resources (Deut. 21) to His firstborn, Israel: "Then say to Pharaoh, 'This is what the LORD says: Israel is my firstborn son'" (Ex. 4:22). He told them He would give them resources so they could bring the lost back into the Father's house. As God redeemed them, they were to become His partner and redeem others, to literally spend themselves on those outside of the Father's house. Sometimes they did a great job with using those resources for God's purposes; other times they kept all the resources for themselves.

Eventually, God had to have a second "firstborn," and in John 3, we learn He sent Jesus with all the resources of the Father for one purpose—to bring back His lost children. Jesus died paying an enormous debt to bring the lost home.

Abraham is a classic example of a patriarch. My favorite Abraham story is in Genesis 18, when he noticed three strangers standing near "his tent in the heat of the day" (v. 1). We can read it's two angels and God, but Abraham only saw three strangers and got up to run toward them. The chapter before, he had been circumcised, so you have to imagine that running was a great physical discomfort. Plus, old men only ran three times in the Bible. It's undignified. He was willing to be shamed and be in pain *for strangers.*

He told Sarah, his wife, to "get three *seahs* of flour" (v. 6). Three *seahs* measure between fifty and seventy-five pounds! How much bread would that make? A lot more than they needed. He did this for three strangers he would never see again because he had his Father's heart for those on the outside.

Where could the Enemy have entered this story? He could've whispered to Abraham to stay seated ("Take care of yourself"), or created a fear of scarcity that worked against generosity ("If you give all that away, what will be left for you?"), or caused division in his marriage ("Abraham, you are crazy! We can't do that").

How does the Enemy come against me in storylines like this? I worry if it will end how I want, if I will look foolish, if I will be misunderstood, if I won't have enough. And instead of responding to the stranger, alien, widow, orphan, or imprisoned, I stay busy talking, protesting, fighting, and posting about issues rather than actually baking bread.

Jesus told a parable in Matthew 13:33, "The kingdom of heaven is like yeast that a woman took and mixed into about sixty pounds of flour until it worked all through the dough." Jesus was telling an audience who knew this story from Genesis: the kingdom of heaven, which I came to bring, is just like Sarah and Abraham, who spent *everything to bring lost people home.* We have an enemy who understands if he can stop us from unselfishly pursuing people outside of the kingdom, he wins.

I have a friend who doesn't share my faith but whom I have spent time with over a number of years. It can feel like I am not getting through, as if it is a waste of time even trying. It's my equivalent to baking three *seahs* of bread. I am hoping that at some point, my behavior or generosity will be shocking enough to prompt questions as to where my kindness comes from. If it never comes, and my efforts never result how I want, it's okay. I am listening and exercising my spiritual muscle of pursuit and sacrifice. It's orienting to know where I am headed and to practice pointing it out to others. God doesn't want anyone to feel lost or that they don't belong because of where they've been or what they've done. He's been hanging out with the controversial and the unclean for a long time:

> Now the tax collectors and sinners were all gathering around to hear Jesus. But the Pharisees and the teachers of the law muttered, "This man welcomes sinners and eats with them."
>
> Then Jesus told them this parable: "Suppose one of you has a hundred sheep and loses one of them. Doesn't he leave the ninety-nine in the open country and go after the lost sheep until he finds it? And when he finds it, he joyfully puts it on his shoulders and goes home. Then he calls his friends and neighbors together and says, 'Rejoice with me; I have found my lost sheep.' I tell you that in the same way there will be more rejoicing in heaven over one sinner who repents than over ninety-nine righteous persons who do not need to repent." (Luke 15:1–7)

God doesn't want anyone to feel lost or that they don't belong because of where they've been or what they've done.

The sheep couldn't find its way back on its own; it is dumb and defenseless. It needs a Shepherd to be out looking for it. The chapter goes on to talk about a woman who lost a coin and searched for it until she found it:

> And when she finds it, she calls her friends and neighbors together and says, "Rejoice with me; I have found my lost coin." In the same way, I tell you, there is rejoicing in the presence of the angels of God over one sinner who repents. (Luke 15:9–10)

There's an emerging pattern: The coin could not have found itself. The woman had to look for it. And rejoicing happens when lost things are found.

One time our son Evan was seemingly lost. As a preschooler, he and his sister had been playing in a tennis court, using it like a giant playpen, while I was standing outside enjoying conversation at the park with our church family. Every few minutes, I would turn and check on them, hearing them laugh and play as they chased a ball. When I turned around and only saw our daughter, I panicked. I yelled to Todd, and for the first five minutes, just he and I were looking. However, within fifteen minutes, the whole church had joined the search, yelling Evan's name and spreading out over the park. At one point, I was walking through a creek, thigh high in water, looking for his body. I was literally a madwoman on the hunt for him.

Then someone shouted to get my attention, and I saw Evan walking down the path with one of our foster daughters. She had taken him to the corner store to buy some chips and, new to the whole family-dynamic thing, she hadn't let us know where they had gone.

I honestly didn't recover for a day or so, and then it started to sink in: God looks for *us* like that. He enlists others, and He walks through metaphorical muddy creeks for us. There is great comfort in imagining God hunting for me (and those I love) with the same passion I had that day.

Luke 15 concludes with the story of a lost son, and even though we call it the story of the "prodigal," there were really two lost sons. I can recognize myself in both their situations: one takes his inheritance and spends it on himself, and the other is entitled and self-righteous. It doesn't matter how we get lost or what condition God finds us in, the Father moves toward us, as the father did for both lost sons, and offers relationship and unconditional love. From the pattern established by the earlier two parables, we know something would be lost (and unable to find itself) and there would be rejoicing when the Shepherd, woman, or Father found it. In case I am still wondering, here it is all spelled out for me: I didn't find myself; God came for me and rejoiced when I was found.

The Devil wants me to feel like no one is looking for me and while there are ninety-nine people partying together, I am not included. Or he wants me panicked about someone I love who is lost, and maybe I am even angry because it seems God has forgotten about my loved one. Our weapon is the truth, and God is clearly telling us in Luke 15: He is coming for us; He is looking for our loved ones.

When the prodigal son walked home, what did the father do? He ate with him—a son who'd been shamed and humbled. The father suffered humiliation to do so. And now we are back to the beginning of the chapter where Jesus was eating with sinners.

Jesus was doing exactly what the father did in the story—hurrying to meet sinners coming toward Him before they even realized how much grace was available, and eating with them, a sign of acceptance and even protection. The father was even kind to the older brother: "'My son,' the father said, 'you are always with me, and everything I have is yours'" (v. 31).

Wherever sin takes me, and whichever brother's lost attitude most resonates (*I want to do it my way* or *How come nothing is credited to me?*), the Bible's message is clear: God rejoices to bring us home. Who we are and where we've been and how we're lost, it doesn't scare Him.

When was the last time you felt spiritually disoriented?

What can you do when you feel lost?

Who spent their resources to bring you into God's family?

Do you relate more with the prodigal son or the older brother?

Chapter 13

Satan wants to dim my light.

God says, "Shine!"

"Listen to me, you who pursue righteousness and who
seek the LORD: Look to the rock from which you were cut
and to the quarry from which you were hewn."
Isaiah 51:1

As a senior in high school, I was a cheerleader for the football team. For homecoming weekend, I was a part of the homecoming court, which required me to change from my uniform into a gown for halftime. Several of my friends and I rode on the backs of cars and, for ten minutes, lived out our childhood princess fantasies. I was as surprised as anyone when they called my name and placed a crown behind the big, early-nineties bangs I had carefully arranged and hair-sprayed.

After taking pictures on the sideline, I hurried to the bathroom to change back into my uniform and was running late. In a huge rush, I checked quickly in the mirror before heading back down to the field to cheer, but I didn't notice the crown still buried underneath my permed hair. As I flew out the door, I ran into Lori, a frenemy who took the opportunity to say, "Oh, take that crown off your head; no one wants to see it on you." Flabbergasted, I reached up, yanked it off my head, and shoved it into my backpack, embarrassed and suddenly full of shame.

Fast-forward fifteen years, and I was in Mexico talking to one of Todd's mentors about an opportunity I was being given to write a book. "I don't know if I will do it. It seems like a lot of work," I said, confusion in my voice.

"I don't know why you wouldn't. Seems like a great move for the ministry, and something you would enjoy. Why are you hesitating?"

I offered some lame excuses, but each time, he pressed a little more. I was getting agitated, clearly having some emotion stirred.

"I've heard you tell some good stories about your life in Mexico. How is this different? Just this time you'd be writing them down," he said.

"Well, why me? Everyone here"—I gestured around, referencing other staff working within our vicinity—"they have good stories too. What makes me the right one to tell them?"

"They asked *you*, that's why." He stated it so matter-of-factly.

"No one wants to see that crown up on my head," I blurted, shocked as it was coming out of my mouth.

"What are you talking about?" he asked, confused by my outburst and brimming tears.

"Oh *wow* ..." I closed my eyes. Silence hung for a moment as realization dawned on me. "I can't believe it. This is about Lori." I shook my head and continued, "I assigned her words to my voice. I almost said no to *this* because of *that*."

He still didn't know what I was talking about, but suddenly I did. The Enemy had used the shame those words created in me to fashion a spiritual bruise. In that spot, he had quietly built a nest, waiting for the right moment to use it against me. He had won that night years ago, and then every time since, I'd shrunk back or dialed down, like a dimmer switch, the light God put inside me.

Recognizing God's light in us isn't conceited or an act of vanity; it's acknowledging we have gifts He's given us and experiences we can testify to, and the result of showing and testifying is spiritual fruit.

When I look back at all the ways God used the book I released the next year, *Reckless Faith*, in my life and our ministry, it takes my breath away. I almost missed it because of a crown, someone else's insecurity, and a healthy dose of unresolved shame.

> For though we live in the world, we do not wage war as the world does. The weapons we fight with are not the weapons of the world. On the contrary, they have divine power to demolish strongholds. We demolish arguments and every pretension that sets itself up against the knowledge of God, and we take captive every thought to make it obedient to Christ. (2 Cor. 10:3–5)

In the book of Joshua, we read about a character named Rahab, who set a lasting example of faith even though she was a prostitute in a family unfamiliar with God. In her story, Joshua sent two spies to check out her city, Jericho, and meet her in the brothel to hide out. It was a good place, since no one looked each other in the eye and likely wouldn't admit they were there.

But the spies weren't very good at their job, because almost immediately the King of Jericho was told, "Look, some of the Israelites have come here tonight to spy out the land." So he sent this message to Rahab: "Bring out the men who came to you and entered your house, because they have come to spy out the whole land" (2:2–3). She reported that the men had already left but if they hurried, they might be able to catch them.

But Rahab had hidden them under stalks of flax she had laid out on the roof. (I like her; she's feisty!) At this point, what can we guess about who Rahab was? She must have been desperate to take up prostitution. She was likely a risk taker, because she hid the spies under threat of her own punishment. She was intuitive and could tell there was something different about these men. And she was smart for reasons we are about to read.

Rahab went to the spies and said, "I know your God is real. I've heard what He did at the Red Sea, of what's happened since" (see 2:8–10). She had ridiculous faith for someone who didn't know God, believing when it cost her something, when no one else around her believed. Imagine how the Enemy whispered in her ear that, because of her profession, she had no value.

> "Now then, please swear to me by the LORD that you will
> show kindness to my family, because I have shown kindness
> to you. Give me a sure sign that you will spare the lives of
> my father and mother, my brothers and sisters, and all who
> belong to them—and that you will save us from death."
> "Our lives for your lives!" the men assured her. "If you
> don't tell what we are doing, we will treat you kindly and
> faithfully when the LORD gives us the land." (2:12–14)

She ended up letting them down by a rope through a window and told them to go to the hills and hide for three days until they could return. Usually when we read in our Bibles about something happening in three days, it means salvation. "They brought out her entire family and put them in a place outside the camp of Israel.... And she lives among the Israelites to this day" (6:23, 25).

There is a lot we don't know about her life after that, but I am sure it changed dramatically as she gained respect among her birth family and her newly adopted tribe. She married a man named Salmon (some believe one of the spies), presumably a Jew since the only others who were saved were her family. He noticed her and pursued her outside of the camp. She was different from everyone else, but he listened and obeyed. After she married, God saw it fit to conceive in her a boy, whom they named Boaz. God knew what was coming.

How did a former prostitute (and a spy?) create a position of respect and high standing for their son? God did that, and it marked the beginning of the blessings of a thousand generations. He completely changed a family's trajectory, just as He does today. The Enemy hates it when a family line is redeemed. And he doesn't go away quietly; he works to remind them of their beginnings so they'll stay there. Imagine how bright Rahab's light must have shined after she rescued her family and God rescued her.

Fast-forward: their son Boaz grew up, and in Ruth 2:1, we learn right away that he was respected: "Now Naomi had a relative on her husband's side, a man of standing from the clan of Elimelek, whose name was Boaz." Boaz saw Ruth in the field, a widow, gathering leftover grain for survival. What went through his mind when he noticed her? We know he instructed his employees not to touch her and told her as much (v. 9); plus, he gave her freedom to collect as much wheat and water as she needed. Wouldn't his mother be so proud! As the lore of her life was told over and over again in his presence growing up, don't you think she explained her previous occupation as her only option? I think after she revealed to him who she was and what she did to survive, she told him about the God who was merciful. This is how God wins. He uses the hard in our histories to nurture empathy for others.

That day in the field, Ruth could hardly believe it and asked, "Why have I found such favor in your eyes that you notice me—a foreigner?" (v. 10). Little did she know that Boaz himself was bicultural, someone who always lived a bit outside the inner circle. He extended to other foreigners the kind of compassion and grace that was at one time extended to his mother. Rahab must have whispered in his ear a thousand times how God had protected them. He developed a compassion for single women, especially those in desperate situations. It was a part of his worldview, his understanding of how the Lord operated.

The love story continues throughout the book, with Boaz working behind the scenes at times to provide for and protect Ruth, and Boaz eventually took her as his wife (4:13). Then Boaz went to Ruth and the Lord enabled her to conceive, and she later gave birth to a son. In this family, we see traits of leadership, boldness, passion, and compassion. These are bright light shiners—world changers. Whether circumstances of prostitute or widow, or cultural differences, they didn't shrink back; their histories and identities made them stronger.

Boaz and Ruth named their son Obed, and he became the father to Jesse. Jesse was the father of David, a risk taker much like his great-grandparents Boaz and Ruth and great-great-grandparents Rahab and Salmon. By the time the family lore had been passed down to David, he had heard many stories of how the God of Israel had come through for his family over and over. It was no wonder at such a young age he picked up a slingshot and some stones to slay a giant. No light dimming there!

If we stopped the story here, it might look like it's easy to shine your light if you have the right family, but that's not true. Each generation has to make a choice: what they will do with what they've been given and their experiences.

Solomon was the son of the powerful king David—a natural light shiner. He was privileged, passionate, wise, rich … What did he do with all these qualities? At one point he was on the right track, but then he married foreigners and allowed compromise in his life and kingdom. And it destroyed everything. The story of his father, David, is fascinating because while he, too, struggled with sin, and another son born out of wedlock was evidence of it, he was quick to repent, and for this God called him a "man after his own heart" (1 Sam. 13:14). God is not expecting our perfection, but He is looking for repentance. Solomon's downfall was that he wouldn't repent. A light can't shine when it is busy hiding sin.

Rahab fought her unseen enemy, and a whole family's future was changed; in fact, Jesus would one day be born from David's line. She lived her life with passion, faith, and risk, and much resulted from her light shining all the way up. If Rahab had kept her mouth shut and listened to what author Dr. Curt Thompson calls our "shame attendant,"[7] what might have been lost? In contrast, unbelievably bright-light Solomon gave in to the Enemy and a whole kingdom was lost.

I've never been more cognizant of how high the stakes are to use the light and life God gave me. I do think about my strengths and weaknesses, my choices and how they affect future generations, but perhaps not enough. What has happened before me? I have great-grandparents whose lives and decisions to keep their light shining impact me today, even though I never met them.

Lydia Sherman was born in 1885 into a family of unbelievers. While a teenager, she came to know Christ as her personal Savior, and her father almost disowned her for it. Undaunted, she graduated in 1912 from Cleveland Bible Institute, now Malone University, determined to enter the ministry. The following year she married Martin Brantingham, also a minister, and they began a church-planting ministry in rural northern Ohio. The family lore is Martin had the gift of helps and used his gift to serve farmers with their chores on the weekend, creating margin for them to attend a service. My great-grandmother Lydia was the stronger preacher and would deliver the messages.

I am sure one reason I am unafraid to fill a pulpit and shine my light is because someone taught someone, who taught someone, who taught me: women can divide the Scripture with authority. My great-grandmother only impacted "so many" people (no megachurches, no internet, no book deals), but her faithfulness and passion set an example for me. I can only imagine how many times the Enemy wanted her to fall or shrink back and, if she had, how that would have impacted my life today.

Our life and obedience are a part of a long story, and our choices and strength fuel the fire of future generations. Some of us are living a Jesus life on top of the shoulders of others. We should live like it. God says we are grafted into His family tree, which means God's family is our family. We've all been cut from His quarry, "the rock from which you were cut," and we can have the blessings of a thousand generations. It can fall on us and our children and their children.

Last weekend my three grandchildren were visiting, and I thought of how they are the great-great-great-granddaughters of Lydia, their mamas grafted into my tree and now growing in an environment of reckless faith. They are hearing my stories and I am confessing my sin, sharing how to repent of temptation and how to pursue God, and how to keep our lights up and on. I can't picture *my* great-great-great-grandchildren, but I am convinced my life will impact theirs. My choices can't be made on how I feel on any given day, but how I want to be a part of an old, long story of faithful light bearers.

> My choices can't be made on how I feel on any given day, but how I want to be a part of an old, long story of faithful light bearers.

Whether we are the Rahab, the first-generation believer making decisions that will be felt many generations later, or we are the beneficiary of others living out their faith for us as an example, this is war and we have to live like it. The apostle Paul describes our struggles with Satan in militaristic terms: "Fight the good fight of the faith" (1 Tim. 6:12). God is rescuing people from "the dominion of darkness" and placing them in His kingdom (Col. 1:13). What we do, how we live, and whether we hide our lights have implications greater than the day we are living in. The way we face our enemy, step up and out, take risks, address shame, speak up, and wage in this war impacts generations.

Do you have a memory of someone telling you to be smaller? What can you do when you feel like shrinking?

What family stories get retold in your family?

How much do you think about your strengths and weaknesses, your choices, and how they impact future generations?

Chapter 14

Satan wants me too weary to fight back.

God strengthens me.

"Therefore we do not lose heart. Though outwardly we are wasting away, yet inwardly we are being renewed day by day."
2 Corinthians 4:16

Some friends of mine adopted a challenging sibling set and have worked remarkably over the years to love and serve their girls. The circumstances the girls were born into and the hand they were dealt could make even those strong in their faith doubt the sovereignty of God. Why do hard things happen to defenseless children? Loving these children over the course of the last decade has cost my friends more than they bargained for. I wonder sometimes if it's all just too much.

Another friend loves a spouse who struggles with addiction. He's in recovery at the moment, but it'll be a lifelong struggle. It requires a constant vigilance and willingness to make sacrificial decisions so he won't be in positions of temptation. There is a cycle of watchfulness, being careful not to be suspicious, then grace when a failing occurs. I can see the weariness in her, and I sometimes wonder how she keeps going.

133

We weren't created to have more relationships than what fits in a village, or more news than impacts one community; it's too much for us to metabolize. However, with the dawn of technology and smartphones, suddenly I have expectations on myself to keep up with friendships way beyond my village, and I have information about tragedies and crises from all over the world. *How do I emotionally, mentally, and spiritually prioritize all those expectations and absorb the pain of that many people? How does it impact my own reserves for the inevitable challenges of daily rhythm and relationships?*

We weren't created to have more relationships than what fits in a village, or more news than impacts one community.

What the Enemy is bargaining on in all of these scenarios is our limited capacity. He knows we can't handle all that's thrown at us, and eventually, we'll lean on protective strategies to cope. Our choices: come to Jesus for direction on how to edit our schedules, ask Him for some supernatural reserves, or go to outside resources. Those outside resources might be some*one* or some*thing* else, but going to anything outside of God that earns our affection and fills us up is idolatry. And once we find relief in our idols, the Enemy wins. He knows applying pressure to our lives will drive us to our idols and separate us from God.

I've had plenty of seasons when compassion, fatigue, or overcommitment issues have driven me to find relief in food, drink, shopping, sleep—it's not hard to want a quick fix. While food, drink, shopping, and sleep aren't inherently evil, if they are being used to prop me up versus allowing God to transform or heal me, then the kingdom loses.

We as a culture are chronically tired, and it's always easier to settle for a quick nap and keep going than deep spiritual rest. But sometimes what we interpret as fatigue is actually something more sinister. In fact, we can wear our exhaustion as badges of honor, when really, they are hiding sin. Here's an example: During COVID-19, we faced many losses (freedom, opportunities, expectations, experiences), and there was an overall sense of heaviness in the culture. You could see it in the grocery store, read it on social media feeds, and hear it in the voices of our family members. But what we were actually feeling was a vague sense of grief; we didn't like what was happening and we weren't sure what was within our power to control. The grief mounted until it bubbled up in pockets within culture and the result was exploding families and city riots.

Todd and I were sharing a meal with some friends during that season, and the wife said her counselor had told her grief was like poop: we need to do a little every day or else we become emotionally constipated. I instantly latched on to that idea and started wondering how much else was building up in me that I was preferring to ignore rather than pass.

Was disappointment or envy, competition or pride building within stories I didn't like and couldn't control, until I was literally exhausted and unable to spiritually fight? I craved more self-awareness. How could I tell the truth when I was afraid? Or sad? Or anxious? What did that kind of daily confession look like, and would practicing it change my emotional fatigue in a way that any treat I might give myself couldn't?

I started to be brutally honest—at first just with myself and God. I would say aloud or write down statements like these:

- I am afraid they think I am better at something than I really am. I might disappoint them.

- I want something that isn't mine. I will delight when someone else enjoys it.
- I am anxious about (this child's) future. I can't control what happens to them.
- I am sad ... or I am mad ... or I am ...

Soon, instead of bringing shame (*I can't believe I am feeling/thinking/wanting this*), the confessions I would've rather not made, when confessed, brought lightness. My friend's counselor was right: like a bowel movement, it was stinky coming out but necessary. Confession looked like grieving (a broken heart over where I had fallen), and grieving looked like confession (sorry, Lord, for longing for what *isn't*). With all the grieving and confession came the unintended benefit of capacity. I want more capacity, because capacity increases impact. When I am not carrying what isn't mine to carry, I have more room in my heart and mind and hands to hold what God entrusts to me.

Todd and I have some friends who are Indian and have been serving the Lord in India for fifty years. We met Dr. John and Jayamani through Back2Back and have spent time in their home and at their dinner table. They have prayed with us and over us and are the kind of people you feel honored to even know, let alone call friends. One time they were in the US visiting their children and made time for us to have dinner. They were telling us about their schedules, dreams, and travel plans. I was exhausted just listening to them, and they are thirty years older than we are!

Finally, I asked with all sincerity, "I have a question for you. I can see you love each other; I can tell you love the Lord, and I hear your heart still for the lost. How do you do it? How are you not waning? Some days I am not sure I can keep going, but you have done more and for longer ... what's your secret?"

I knew there wasn't a secret, and in some ways, I imagined they would hear the question as rhetorical. Dr. John looked me right in the eye and said with complete sincerity, "Jayamani and I start our day with hours of prayer."

I looked at him skeptically. *"Hours?"*

His wife laughed, then clarified, "He does it three hours; I am weaker, so for me it's probably more like two hours, but we awaken early and spend time with God, asking Him for strength and wisdom. We are getting older and need more and more of His strength and wisdom. Discernment and spiritually prioritizing the day are our highest concerns."

I sat back in my chair, knowing what was available to them was available to me. Why when I am thirsty do I drink Diet Coke rather than water? Why when I am drained of sitting, thinking, or just being, do I stay in stasis when my body would benefit from moving? Why when I am tired do I see spiritual activity as one more thing to do, rather than the life-saving, life-altering action of someone who understands we are, first, spiritual beings?

Dr. John and Jayamani were living a supernatural life, and it was inspiring. In 2 Corinthians 4:16, we read, "Therefore we do not lose heart. Though outwardly we are wasting away, yet inwardly we are being renewed day by day." When our passion outruns our wisdom, someone always gets hurt. That is what can happen when I don't stop to process what I am doing or what I've been through. When I don't rest although I'm tired, think before I say yes, or am too busy to see what's coming for me, I am spiritually vulnerable.

It's one of Satan's most effective tactics: if we are too tired doing what we *think* we are supposed to, or what *someone else* thinks we are supposed to, then we don't see what God has for us. Suddenly, the idea of rest shifted from a "time-out" (which I have never liked) to being a weapon I could use in my war against sin. God invites us into a rhythm where He is our deep breath. Time in rest fortifies us for the fight and the life He's called us to; it's not a sign of tapping out, but gearing up. Rest is *not* lack of activity, but a still heart.

How can you tell you are feeling spiritually weary? What can you do about it?

What would a list of brutally honest statements from you look like?

What are you grieving?

What's the difference between available and busy?

Chapter 15

Satan wants me judgmental and unaware of my own sin.

God gives freedom.

"Why do you look at the speck of sawdust in your brother's
eye and pay no attention to the plank in your own eye?"
Matthew 7:3

Someone asked me the other day how the planning was going for our daughter's wedding. As I shared a few details, I could tell I was looking for the woman's approval. As if "liking a post" from social media had seeped its way into our conversation, and her head nod was the equivalent to a thumbs-up. I didn't need her to be excited about charcuterie boards or wedding favors, yet weirdly, I did. Every day, we are asked our opinions. We comment on someone else's photos on social media, we review restaurants, we add product reviews, we blog, we op-ed, we speak out on just about *everything*. All that evaluation can create in us a sense of us against them, or my way is better. It's divisive and can leave us prideful or bitter or self-righteous.

I have long struggled in this area: having opinions about how people talk or dress or act or parent or spend or a whole bunch of other things that are none of my business. I asked God for a breakthrough in my life in this area, and I am happy to testify that He provided some major pivots that started me out of this pattern of thinking. Now I just have to keep reminding myself what I learned.

The first was a study I did called *Gospel Transformation*, written for missionaries going to serve overseas. I wasn't sure what I was in for, but some friends and I sat down to examine our vulnerabilities. Through this season I recognized I had fallow ground that needed confessing.

> Sow for yourselves righteousness;
>   reap steadfast love;
>   break up your fallow ground. (Hos. 10:12 ESV)

"Fallow ground" means unconfessed sin. Although confession brings freedom, it is easier to defend an unhealthy pattern than confess it. It requires identifying the log in my own eye and realizing how much it interferes with my life. When I recognize how broken I am, I lose the "umph" to judge others. While judgment destroys a relationship, or at least the level of intimacy a relationship can experience, confession disarms the other person and refreshingly invites connection.

> Do not judge, or you too will be judged. For in the same way you judge others, you will be judged, and with the measure you use, it will be measured to you.
>
> Why do you look at the speck of sawdust in your brother's eye and pay no attention to the plank in your own eye? How can you say to your brother, "Let me take the speck out of your eye," when all the time there is a plank in your own eye? (Matt. 7:1–4)

We are an awfully divided culture—choosing sides based on our color, sports teams, school choices, politics—the list is infinite. Division stems from judgment and is authored by our adversary. Unity, on the other hand, reflects the heart of Jesus and validates the gospel. It's expensive, not driven by compromise, and involves sacrifice. Jesus spent a lot to unite us, and we toss that aside when we size one another up and determine if one of us is left wanting. The chorus of judgment sings "My way is better than your way" or "My people are better than your people." We are desperate for our way to be the right way of thinking, because it satisfies our sense of justice and our feelings of shame.

Even with the work I've done to experience freedom from judgment, I can still struggle. The moment I engage in evaluative thinking, the Enemy has found the soft spot he is looking for to get my eyes off Jesus and onto others or myself. Bonus points for him if I open my mouth and start talking about it. Then I gossip or criticize or envy. We can see the Church or culture extend itself in generous and sacrificial ways, and still have thoughts we shouldn't and enter into debates that are none of our business.

> I therefore, a prisoner for the Lord, urge you to walk in a manner worthy of the calling to which you have been called, with all humility and gentleness, with patience, bearing with one another in love, eager to maintain the unity of the Spirit in the bond of peace. (Eph. 4:1–3 ESV)

In the Greek, "eager" could be translated as "spare no effort." Whatever you need to do, do it to be free of what divides us. It takes awareness, confession, and discipline to walk in freedom.

The other teaching that played a key role in removing my log was from biblical scholar N. T. Wright.[8] Since God brought peace into the chaos of the world, then I, too, am to be a peace bringer, not a chaos contributor. From judgment erupts chaos, either inside my heart or out my mouth. The question I ask myself now when I see chaos is *Will I sit in judgment of someone else's choices, or will I bring a measure of God's peace and understanding to their story?* Judgment keeps me in chaos, and it's a strategy of the Enemy that is effective individually and in groupthink. How many denominations of the Church are there today, and how do they feel about one another?

If I think poorly of someone, focusing only on the person's faults, or even worse, judging an entire life by its weakest moments, then I am emulating evil. It's sinful to judge the assumed motives of others without considering myself in their same circumstances. All that judging is exhausting and was never intended to be my burden to carry. I can show unconditional love without showing unconditional *approval*. God says it over and over again: I am to love, period.

> I can show unconditional love without showing unconditional approval.

We don't have to walk around with logs in our eyes. We get to live free: free to confess our sin, free to want the best for others, free to come to Jesus, free to love and give away that freedom to others. I am God's kid, and yet, I can still live with a lack of understanding who my spiritual Father is and how life as His kid unfolds. The sin of judgment is born out of a need to be better than someone else in order to feel accepted, but living inside His family should so fill me up that I have plenty to spill over to others.

I understand my identity best when I spend time with God and I learn who He says I am. God invites me to live as His kid and, with this liberty, bring peace to others. It's with the kind of sweet freedom felt after a hard-fought battle that I can sincerely look around and say, "You work out your faith at your own pace and directly with God. Judgment is no longer a stronghold for me. I am too busy looking in the mirror, plucking out my own planks."

Who or what do you most frequently judge?

Where do you have fallow ground? What can you do about it?

How much confession is in your daily spiritual rhythm?

Chapter 16

Satan wants me numb.

God wakes me up.

"Then [Jesus] returned to his disciples and found them sleeping.
'Simon,' he said to Peter, 'are you asleep? Couldn't you keep
watch for one hour? Watch and pray so that you will not fall
into temptation. The spirit is willing, but the flesh is weak.'"
Mark 14:37-38

When I sit too long in one position, my foot falls asleep and it ends up feeling numb. That's what falling spiritually asleep feels like, numbness. What I once cared about, I don't so much anymore. I am tired of waiting. Tired of working. Tired of wanting something to be one way. It's all too much … exhausting. And I wonder if I just close my eyes for a second, if there's some relief.

During one season I was traveling so much that when I landed somewhere, sometimes I wasn't sure where I was. At an airport late one night, I discovered my flight was delayed three hours and I was so yearning to get on board and just fall asleep. I needed relief from my fatigue, so I looked around at my options, knowing I couldn't keep my eyes open one more minute. I spotted a family restroom—the larger ones with a single stall and a lock on the door. *Yes!* I slipped inside and curled up on the floor, feeling safe behind the lock as I drifted off to sleep. Now I think how gross that was, but at the time it felt like such relief.

The Enemy wants me to be numb and to coast. His goal is for me to feel like it's all just *too* much work—too overwhelming—and I can't keep up with the demands. He would love if I got lazy and inattentive, allowing small problems to become big problems. Whatever the type of maintenance, whether it's house, car, or relationship, when warning signs go off, they need attention or something breaks down. *Just let me metaphorically close my eyes for a second; surely I deserve it.* But a second is all he needs.

Jesus was pressing into this in the Garden of Gethsemane when He asked Simon Peter, "Are you asleep?" He had taken three of the disciples (Peter, James, and John) into the garden, but He asked this question of Peter. He was sending a warning sign that a small problem was going to become a big problem, and was he willing to stay alert?

Peter is interesting to study because he has several distinct chapters in his faith journey, and the Enemy, who uses the same tricks over and over, reveals his unique strategies depending on our soul's condition. Before Peter was called to be a disciple, we have to imagine how the Enemy might have attacked him since it isn't recorded. In the disciple period, we can study all kinds of enemy counteractivity: when he was walking on water and seeing miracles and the time in the garden when he fell asleep. Finally, there was his out-of-control stage of cutting off the guard's ear and denying Christ three times.

Peter has been through it with Jesus. It's one of the reasons I love studying him. *I* have been through it with Jesus too; most of us have. My faith journey has not been a straight line; sometimes it has looked like a figure eight. Like Peter, I have been taught, challenged, and edified by Christ. I have seen God's power, but I am no longer naive enough to think following Him means a constant upward growth trajectory without missteps and setbacks. After Peter saw miracles like the feeding of the five thousand and dead people rising, what would cause him who was once awake to fall asleep?

We each have seasons when it all becomes too much and we sleepwalk through them. It can then take someone else to point out that we are asleep for us to notice. One of our Back2Back staff members, Rick, was giving a driving lesson to a teen we work with in the urban area of our city. Taking advantage of the time together for conversations about the teen's life, dreams, and thoughts, Rick asked him what he was planning to do after high school.

"Well, I already finished last year. I passed all my classes, but I didn't pay my school fees, so they are withholding my diploma. I can't really plan on anything until I get that." The student's future was being held up by an unpaid school fee? That seemed crazy—totally resolvable. But fighting an inflexible system can leave you fatigued and numb. When Rick told this story, I was both grateful we could get involved in a solution and self-reflective. *What have I become okay with that isn't okay?*

Peter fell asleep in a garden called Gethsemane (Mark 14:32–37), which means "olive press." Jesus was also pressed. The great weight of the sin of the world led Him to sweat drops of blood. He didn't want anyone to be numb about what was going to happen. He needed them alert to witness that He was about to be crushed. What came out of pressed olives? Olive oil, which was used for anointing and for lanterns, very fitting for the One who was called the "Light of the World" and the "Anointed One."

"Your word is a lamp to my feet and a light to my path" (Ps. 119:105 ESV). When the psalmist wrote that verse, he was referring to a lamp of the time, with a wick probably giving off the light equivalent to a birthday candle. When God promises His light will illuminate my path, I picture a light with a twenty-five-foot beam. I want the confidence of seeing way out in the distance, but the light God promises might only be enough for me to see the next step. If I get lazy or fatigued and stop growing—by reading the Word and asking God for guidance—I will step into the darkness, exactly what my enemy wants.

For example, I want to see ahead into high-stakes circumstances to know the results of my actions. I want to know where I am going to end up, and then I'll decide if it's worth the journey. I lack the faith to believe obedience will bring an awaited blessing. When Todd and I took in twin foster daughters twenty years ago, I had no idea they would end up giving us a lifetime of joy and granddaughters we now love. God only showed me that ride one step at a time; He wanted me to grow through the uncertainty.

In this garden, feeling pressed, knowing what was going to happen, Jesus told His disciples, "Sit here while I pray" (Mark 14:32). And then He "fell to the ground and prayed that if possible the hour might pass from him. 'Abba, Father,' he said, 'everything is possible for you. Take this cup from me. Yet not what I will, but what you will'" (vv. 35–36).

When I pray like that, sharing how I really feel, "Take this cup from me" (whatever the cup is in that season), and still align with Him, "Yet not what I will, but what you will," I look most like Jesus. If I try to put my best spiritual foot forward, it never works. He knows who I am and how I am feeling. It's better when I just say, "I don't like this; take it from me, but if You don't, it's okay."

Have you ever sat with someone who was going through something unbearable? A medical procedure? A breakup? A funeral? I sat in court with a friend who was in the middle of a horrific custody battle, and it was hard to stay present. The idea of closing my eyes for a minute held great appeal. However, by repeating this truth from the garden, "Yet not what I will, but what you will," I released control over something I had no ability to change, and I could stay present, even alive, in a posture of trust.

I have to let go of control, because trying to be in control is exhausting; and confess my sin, because holding on to sin is exhausting; and be present, because worrying about tomorrow is exhausting. Maybe it seems like staying spiritually in shape is exhausting, but it's actually less work than the alternative, which is dealing with the fallout of a life destroyed by sin.

Maybe it seems like staying spiritually in shape is exhausting, but it's actually less work than the alternative.

"Then [Jesus] returned to his disciples and found them sleeping. 'Simon,' he said to Peter, 'are you asleep? Couldn't you keep watch for one hour? Watch and pray so that you will not fall into temptation. The spirit is willing, but the flesh is weak'" (Mark 14:37–38). Jesus wanted him to stay awake *for Peter's sake.* What kind of temptation did He want Peter to resist? Is the same true for me? Does Jesus know what will happen when I get sleepy and unable to resist temptation? He sees how sin will destroy both me and the kingdom He wants to build through me. I am heartsick over Christian leaders who fall in spectacularly public ways. They are no different from anyone else, only the Enemy gets more mileage from their sin. The body, which is weak, overcomes the spirit not weathering well in some storm, and relief in the form of sin becomes too much to fight.

Jesus, being sovereign, knew Peter would deny Him shortly; He sees our whole lives at one time. This is Jesus—*all the time.* He knew what the next three days would be like and He was warning Peter: this time the Exodus will be big; *stay awake.* This was about the redemption of God's people, and He wanted the disciples to be alert so they could remember and testify. When God prompts us to stay "awake," it isn't out of shaming or performance; it's the heart of a Father who doesn't want us to fall asleep at the wheel and crash or miss what He's doing!

When Peter woke up in the garden, he began an out-of-control stage where he cut off the ear of the guard and later denied Christ three times. He was rebellious, angry, and afraid. When we have big feelings, we can forget who we are, making poor choices or acting out of our own weaknesses. I can talk myself into and out of what I normally wouldn't think of doing.

Someone once falsely accused me of something. Todd was with me when the person confronted me, and because he knew it was impossible for me to have done what was claimed, he went ballistic. If Todd had had a sword, he might have cut off the person's ear. He had big feelings of anger and fear and was irrational. *It can happen that fast.* God knows our weaknesses and warns us to stay alert. The Enemy also knows our weaknesses, and wanting kingdom damage, he'll take it anywhere he can get it.

Have you ever asked yourself, *How did I get here? How did it get this bad? When did this even start?* The answer is, something becomes too much and we don't surrender. Then, eventually exhausted, we get numb and fall asleep. Now with the right environment, the Enemy will win.

When I fall asleep figuratively, I let things slide. I don't pay attention to my children, stop parenting, and just manage them. I don't pay attention to my marriage, and we coexist, or worse. I don't pay attention to my calling and instead start building my own kingdoms. I don't pay attention to my tongue, and I speak what I shouldn't. I don't pay attention to my thought life, and I fantasize about what isn't mine. The result of this inattention and slumber is temptation. James tells us temptation leads to sin, and sin to death: "Then, after desire has conceived, it gives birth to sin; and sin, when it is full-grown, gives birth to death" (James 1:15).

When I am out of control, nothing makes sense and I want to quit—out of shame or just fatigue. We can assume Peter thought his actions disqualified him. But in Mark 16:7, it says, "Go get the disciples *and Peter* ..." God has plans for me yet. He isn't put off by my faltering. He knew about Peter's denial, and yet He wanted him. Even when I am irrational, even when I am rebellious, even when I've given up and quit, He wants *me*.

God would go on to use Peter—the sleeping, ear-cutting, denying Peter—in miraculous ways. In Acts 2, Peter spoke in tongues and ushered in the Holy Spirit. He would have woken up that day and celebrated something called *Shavuot* in Hebrew, the remembering of the Ten Commandments the Jewish people received fifty days after Passover. God had a plan to use Peter despite his previous failings, and by the end of that day, "those who accepted his message were baptized, and about three thousand were added to their number that day" (Acts 2:41).

God wants to involve us in His plans. But we have to be awake and alert to His prompting and His will, and then He *will* use us, even after seasons of slumber and rebellion. He restores, redeems, and rebuilds ... we don't want to miss it.

What is an example in your life when a small problem became a big problem?

Have you ever spiritually fallen asleep?

How can you tell when you are numb? What can you do about it?

Chapter 17

Satan wants me anxious.

God is peace.

"Do not be anxious about anything, but in every situation, by prayer and petition, with thanksgiving, present your requests to God. And the peace of God, which transcends all understanding, will guard your hearts and your minds in Christ Jesus."
Philippians 4:6-7

Normally during the day, I think in rainbows and unicorns, but sometimes at night, I can think in terms of catastrophes and lie awake in a state of anxiety. It can involve any number of reasons and topics:

- stuff that hasn't even happened
- stuff that has happened but can't be fixed or changed
- conversations I wish I had had (and then playing out both sides)
- conversations I wish hadn't happened (and then replaying what I wish I would've said instead)
- my children (any of them) in any unfortunate circumstance, past, present, or future
- irrational fears (about my health, finances, husband, etc.)

One night, realizing I needed God, I reached for my phone on my nightstand, careful not to wake Todd. I opened my Bible app and noticed for the first time there was an audio feature, so I hit *play*. I happened to be in the Gospels, so it was mostly Jesus' words. I was in the dark, on the phone, and a man was reading Jesus' words to me … it felt like Jesus was calling me! The Word promises to heal, and after a while, I felt the peace needed to relax and fall back to sleep. Nothing had changed, nothing was fixed, there was just space now created for God to bring His presence.

I can struggle with believing God's truth if I am in a desert, a place where *nothing is going how I want*. I can "feel" like not fighting anxiety or obeying Him or abiding with Him. The Hebrew word for *desert* is *midbar*, which also means "the place of the word." God speaks to us in the place of the word. It was in the desert that God spoke to Abraham, Moses, Isaiah, and even Jesus. When we're in the desert or wilderness, we're closer to God than ever, because it is in the *midbar* that we realize we need God and can trust Him with our anxious thoughts and unclear futures. "Therefore I am now going to allure her; I will lead her into the wilderness and speak tenderly to her" (Hos. 2:14).

I spoke with a church leader last night who was feeling beat up by a storyline the Enemy introduced into his church. This man fought ferociously to protect his community, and in the end, God won. However, now he's exhausted, and he shared with me his desire to resign. "I am not cut out for this," he said.

I gently protested. "This is exactly what the Enemy wants. He still wins if you withdraw, taking with you the lie you weren't enough and 'church' is messed up. What if God was using this story to strengthen your convictions, build your communication skills, and now, although battle weary, you are surer than ever there is a war, and you are on the right side? What if Satan's attempt to take you out just backfired on him, and now you are more experienced and aware of the spiritual warfare swirling around leaders?"

That's what I am hoping for—a spirit of fight in me, a familiarity with spiritual battle, and a boldness to advance against the kingdom of darkness. While we get stirred up and sit in anxious thoughts of *What if?* and *What now?*, the battle is already raging. The Devil is a bully, and if I back down and give up, stay quiet, or don't share truth or testimony, he wins.

I am learning to see the temptation of anxiety for what it is, the beckoning finger of our enemy to walk into a mind trap, ultimately designed to hurt us. When I see him luring me toward foreboding and I face it square on, I save myself future and present pain. Instead of picking myself up off the ground, I want to do the work beforehand to stay at peace so I can be a nonanxious presence in a world that's restless and disturbed. If I need to counterattack the Devil to make it happen, so be it.

I want to use exactly what the Devil is trying against me, and instead use it against him. If I am anxious about a child, I want to invest time in intercession for him or her. If I am anxious about next steps, I want to use the opportunity to reflect on where God has brought me from and the biblical promises He has for my future. Worry is just meditation in the wrong direction. If I can flip the script, I get positive mileage out of whatever is triggering me. If I am worried about my health, I can thank God for how my body is working. If I am worried about money, I can recount past provision and rejoice in how He's provided.

Worry is just meditation in the wrong direction.

When I don't like what's happening, or it seems out of control, I feel helpless. *I can't, I'm not enough* … these thoughts keep me in a pattern of inactivity, or worse yet, *shame*. Then uncomfortable, and in an effort to feel better about myself, I reach for what seems good in the moment. Only offering temporary relief, it leaves me feeling worse afterward, and the cycle continues. These patterns, played out on large and small scales, contribute to the sense I am broken, and when I give up on myself, the Evil One wins.

When he lies, he speaks according to his own nature, "for he is a liar and the father of lies" (John 8:44). In disguise, he breeds doubt of God and of my own worth. In Genesis 3, his first words are disbelieving of the truth: "Did God really say, 'You must not eat from any tree in the garden'?" His second words were deceitful, "You will not certainly die," and he has been lying to us ever since.

There are plenty of familiar biblical characters who had to overcome anxiety: Jonah was anxious about his assignment and ran away, Jeremiah, Nehemiah, King David, Mordecai, Martha was anxious about what her sister left her to do (Luke 10:40–42), and Mary and Joseph were looking for their lost twelve-year-old son:

> After three days they found him in the temple courts, sitting among the teachers, listening to them and asking them questions. Everyone who heard him was amazed at his understanding and his answers. When his parents saw him, they were astonished. His mother said to him, "Son, why have you treated us like this? Your father and I have been anxiously searching for you." (Luke 2:46–48)

Being anxious and worrying are clearly a part of our human journey. So if I can't will it away, how do I fight spiritually against it? Peace comes with the recognition that God is sovereign. The Enemy can use anxious feelings about absolutely anything: our health, the weather, money, our children, the future, the past, the present … and we will be tricked into distraction, thinking the key solution is a plan involving the power of positive thinking or other contingency plans. But Jesus is in control, and if He is writing the story as the "author and perfecter of our faith" (Heb. 12:2 ASV), we can trust it's good. He is God-with-us, and this truth digested brings peace—regardless of circumstances.

- A plane is late … God is with me.
- A test came back positive … God is with me.
- A friendship is strained, a child is wayward, a bank account is low … God is still with me.

What kinds of things make you anxious? What can you do about it?

When was a time you felt in the desert? How did God speak to you there?

Does anxiety sneak up on you or hit you all at once?

What lies are easiest for you to believe?

Chapter 18

Satan wants to confuse my identity.

God provides belonging.

"But if I say, 'I will not mention his word or speak anymore in his name,' his word is in my heart like a fire, a fire shut up in my bones. I am weary of holding it in; indeed, I cannot."
Jeremiah 20:9

Some Back2Back team members and I were on a prayer walk, visiting families who received services at our Tres Reyes Community Center in Cancún, Mexico. At each stop, we'd meet the family and ask how we could pray for them. They'd mention provision, health needs, or broken relationships. Typically the mother would share the most vulnerably, and as we lifted her needs, a fragile connection would form.

As we entered Maria's house, she proudly introduced us to her two elementary-aged children, quick to share their academic successes and credit them for their hard work. When she finished, someone asked how she found out about the center. She laughed. "That is a funny story."

One of the staff met her while walking in the community and encouraged her to enroll her children in tutoring classes. She distrusted Americans and, due to her illiteracy, feared embarrassment if she couldn't fill out forms. She successfully avoided the issue for a while, but with her son falling behind in school, she eventually had nowhere else to turn. One afternoon she came to the community center but insisted on standing outside the classroom while her children participated. Although this meant long hours in the hot sun, she was concerned for her children's safety.

Sandy, one of the teachers, sensed Maria listening to her teach through a window. The next day, she left Maria a chair outside the door, a kind gesture so she could sit while the children were in class. Instead of resting, Maria sat on the edge of her seat. Sandy recognized her attentiveness, as if learning the material for the first time. The next morning on her way into the classroom, Sandy quietly dropped a notebook on Maria's seat.

As Maria told it, the lessons began to make sense. She strung together letters to make words, and then words to read sentences. Eventually, she attended parenting classes, where she learned about cooking, finances, and faith. "I don't want you to tell me what God says about me anymore," she told her Bible class. "Now that I can read, give me a Bible. I want to find out for myself."

"That was three years ago," she said. "And now, I have been baptized, and I share my faith journey regularly with my extended family and neighbors."

Maria's life looks different from just a few years ago. She makes items to sell in the market and competently supports her family. She worships alongside her children. She admitted she is not only working toward a future, but she's also trying to rebuild a broken past. "I was angry and scared, and God had so much waiting for me. Sometimes all we need to turn things around is an invitation."

God says our identity is found in Him, but the Enemy wants us to wear labels as if they are our identities.

> God says our identity is found in Him, but the Enemy wants us to wear labels as if they are our identities.

A child of an alcoholic.

An unwed mother.

A juvenile delinquent.

A liar. A gossip.

A cheater.

Then when we want to step out, or step up, we feel held back by who we are.

Consider the story of Timothy in the Bible. His mother was Eunice, a Jew, and his grandmother was Lois. Eunice's partner was Greek, so their child was a *mamzer*, a person born from certain forbidden relationships.[9] This meant Timothy couldn't go to temple school, and he couldn't sit in synagogue or study the Torah. A rabbi would have told his mom, "Deuteronomy 23:2 says, 'No one born of a forbidden marriage nor any of their descendants may enter the assembly of the LORD, not even in the tenth generation.'" If his mother would have asked the rabbi to have him circumcised, the answer would've been no. (He would be later by Paul.) He couldn't marry anyone but another mamzer. He was the one everyone laughed at. *Your mom was bad.* "Mamzer" would have felt like an identity. (Thanks to Ray Vander Laan for this teaching.)

Timothy's story is inspiring because even with all the limitations he would have faced, we learn from a letter later written to him, "But as for you, continue in what you have learned and have become convinced of, because you know those from whom you learned it, and how from infancy you have known the Holy Scriptures, which are able to make you wise for salvation through faith in Christ Jesus" (2 Tim. 3:14–15).

How is that possible? Did Eunice know the Bible from memory? Did Lois know the Bible? His dad didn't. Is it possible Timothy sat outside the window of the synagogue and listened in the tall grass, or did he listen once a week, when the rabbi would publicly read the Torah on the steps? Somehow this mamzer learned the Scripture. No rabbi would have taken him, ever.

Maria landed in the middle of a community where people were concerned about her family's well-being. She first knew Christians before she knew Christ. They left an impression on her, stoking a curiosity and challenging what she previously thought was true. This is often how it works. The lost will sense God's love through God's people and be moved by it. It's our privilege then to make sure Maria looks through us to God, instead of at us for what we can never provide.

God interrupted what would have been the expected next events of Maria's story to redirect her path. It's what He does. In the Gospels, we read how He saw the Samaritan woman at a well and used her testimony to impact a community. He saw a bleeding woman in need of a touch and drew His attention to her healing. He saw an adulterous woman needing forgiveness and a crowd too critical to offer it, so He reached out. For Maria, He saw a desperate mom needing support, and He sent it through a teacher who offered a chair and a notebook. The Word of God is powerful; it does something in angry single moms and vulnerable mamzer children.

One day, the famous Paul showed up in Timothy's town. Paul was best in class; he wrote thirteen books in the Bible, was a missionary and a revolutionary, and had the best pedigree. As a mamzer, Timothy couldn't be a part of anything associated with Paul. Paul came to this town and was teaching with this fire in his chest. Paul wrote to the Colossians, "Here there is no Gentile or Jew, circumcised or uncircumcised, barbarian, Scythian, slave or free, but Christ is all, and is in all" (Col. 3:11). Perhaps he was saying something similar in Lystra, and could Timothy have been thinking, *Maybe there are no mamzers?*

Paul healed a lame man and the people believed him to be a god. He told them he wasn't, but some stirred up the crowd. "They stoned Paul and dragged him outside the city, thinking he was dead. But after the disciples had gathered around him, he got up and went back into the city" (Acts 14:19–20). Paul demonstrated power: *Stone me and I am coming back.* I believe Paul knew he was at war with darkness. The Enemy was trying to stop him from spreading the gospel, but Paul continued at all costs. I want to be someone not easily deterred, to know so thoroughly who I am that nobody can convince me to change course.

English evangelist Graham Cooke said, "You can tell the quality of someone's inner life by the amount of opposition it takes to discourage them."[10] What was Paul's inner life like? When I am feeling discouraged, I know it's time to strengthen my inner life. How do I do that? Pray, read the Word, sing praise. These are the same tools I have to fight the Enemy, and using them cultivates an inner life that translates like fire.

Nothing would stop Paul! Timothy saw (from outside) this man's message and his passion. Two years passed, and Paul returned to Lystra in Acts 16 on his second teaching tour, where Timothy, a believer, lived. This time when Paul came to town, he was looking for disciples, and Timothy had changed.

Timothy, on his own, learned the text. *How?* Paul must have wondered. It says the believers spoke well of him, so Paul wanted to take him along. "Paul came also to Derbe and to Lystra. A disciple was there, named Timothy, the son of a Jewish woman who was a believer, but his father was a Greek. He was well spoken of by the brothers at Lystra and Iconium" (vv. 1–2 ESV).

Imagine all the boys lined up to be picked by the great Paul. What would you have given to be standing next to Timothy when Paul said, "Hey, are you Timothy? I want you to come with me. I want *you* to be my disciple"?

"You *know* I am a mamzer?"

"There are no mamzers in Jesus."

"Mom! Grandma! Paul wants *me*!"

He was the least likely, and that is God's favorite kind. The next we hear of him is in Paul's letters addressed to him in the biggest city, Ephesus. Paul started his letters "To Timothy my true son," which would have meant the world to him, since Timothy never really had a dad. Paul was committing to stand in the gap as his spiritual dad. "To Timothy, my dear son" (2 Tim. 1:2). He even nagged like a dad, "Timothy, I keep reminding you … Fan the flames, keep it burning" (see v. 6). The same fire Paul had, Timothy had too.

God loves the fire, but the Enemy is afraid of it; it's where he'll one day end up. "And the devil that deceived them was cast into the lake of *fire*"

(Rev. 20:10 KJV). Whereas God has been in pillars of fire, tongues of fire, and burning bushes, and fire is good, for the Devil, the fire is a warning of what's to come.

Timothy lived what the prophet Jeremiah said, "But if I say, 'I will not mention his word or speak anymore in his name,' his word is in my heart like a fire, a fire shut up in my bones. I am weary of holding it in; indeed, I cannot" (Jer. 20:9), and in doing so, he put his identity as God's kid on full display.

I sense God's fire in me every time I am prompted to speak up. This is *chutzpah*, the Hebrew word meaning "utter audacity, nerve." It's bold, compelled to act. Fire is better than "sparkle." People want sparkle these days; they want to be known for their style, but fire and substance are far more compelling and pleasing to God. Paul saw in Timothy this kind of bravery and boldness. Talent and IQ mean nothing without fire. I want to have the fire in my chest and a love for the Word.

The Enemy whispers that our identities are wrapped up in our prosperity or success, which we're lulled into thinking come from our own big ideas. God says those are things He gives when we live His way. "Keep this Book of the Law always on your lips; meditate on it day and night, so that you may be careful to do everything written in it. Then you will be prosperous and successful" (Josh. 1:8). I love a good class or article about strategy, innovation, and disruption. There's a place for business acumen, but don't ever place it over faithfulness. God honors boldness and obedience born from security in who we are.

"Don't let anyone look down on you because you are young, but set an example for the believers in speech, in conduct, in love, in faith and in purity" (1 Tim. 4:12). Someone may look down on me because I am younger, older, richer, poorer, a mamzer, and I can let it limit me. Or I can identify as God's kid, and now the sky is the limit. That limitless, I-can-do-all-things-through-Christ mindset terrifies our adversary. Satan wants us to be held back or down, so every chance, in every conversation, using all of his tricks, he will tempt us and lie to us until we believe we are anything but redeemed. There's a rabbinical saying: plan one thing every day you can't do without God. To fight off the Enemy, make it a habit to punch higher than your class, trying something the world says you can't do, then give God the glory and make Him the star when it happens.

Who do you know who reflects God's light instead of stealing it for himself or herself?

What parts of your life experience do you wear like an identity?

How easily are you discouraged? What can you do about it?

Chapter 19

Satan wants me distracted with pleasure.

God is my Deliverer.

"[The LORD] is my loving God and my fortress, my
stronghold and my deliverer, my shield, in whom I
take refuge, who subdues peoples under me."
Psalm 144:2

My flesh can want and hunger for what isn't mine. I can seek hits with food
or drink, and lust with my eyes and mind. Caught in sin's trap, I am helpless without Christ. Only His ransom will set me free, but the Enemy can
make the trap seem too strong to break. If I am distracted with meeting the
needs of the flesh, I miss out on the opportunity to rely on Jesus, to feel His
victory, and to sacrifice. This adversary, he "prowls around like a roaring
lion looking for someone to devour" (1 Pet. 5:8) but is no match for the
Spirit of the Lord, who can rip him away from me when I call for strength
and rescue. Judges 14:6 says about Samson, "The Spirit of the LORD came
powerfully upon him so that he tore the lion apart with his bare hands as
he might have torn a young goat."

> If I am distracted with meeting
> the needs of the flesh, I miss out on
> the opportunity to rely on Jesus, to
> feel His victory, and to sacrifice.

Steve had worked hard through college and graduate school to set himself up for a career he loved. He married Kelli, a beautiful woman whom everyone admired. They started their climb up the ladder, complete with lavish vacations and second houses. Inside their marriage, however, were cracks: misunderstandings, growing frustrations, and lack of accountability. They thought starting a family might keep them together and renew their commitment to each other. But a struggle with infertility added a new pressure to their already-strained relationship.

Eventually, they did conceive multiple times and grew a large family. However, the years were full of the demands of children, misunderstandings, and unmet needs. The environment was ripe for the Enemy to invade. Where did he start? *Anywhere he could.*

Steve began sleeping in another room to get a full night's sleep for his demanding workdays. He would go to bed feeling lonely, unsatisfied, and trapped. Kelli felt overwhelmed with the responsibility of their growing family and went to bed feeling unsupported, judged, and afraid.

In the mornings, they each worked passively or aggressively for the other spouse to understand their pain. *You don't know how hard it is to be me*, they each thought. Disconnected, he left for work, already not looking forward to coming home. Disconnected, she looked around the house, wondering if anyone really saw her or if everyone just wanted to use her.

At this point, the Enemy could employ any number of tricks to cause their fall or increase their disconnection. His common strategy is to tempt people into something destructive that allows for a moment of pain relief. Because we love pleasure (and there are plenty of God-ordained, healthy ways to experience it), we gravitate toward it. While pleasure means a feeling of happy satisfaction and enjoyment, there is a dark side to it. Pleasure is something we first notice (perception), then we *feel* a sensation from or around it, which causes us to want to make physical contact with what is bringing us pleasure and, finally, to develop a desire to own it. We can want to own a thing, a person, or obtain power, status, or recognition. The more we feed this shadow side, the hungrier it gets, until eventually what's bitter tastes sweet and what's sweet tastes bitter.

Every person is unique, so what will tempt each of us is unique to our individual personalities, backgrounds, and past experiences. The Enemy sees our history and family patterns and dangles the perfect carrots in front of our noses. For Kelli, she needed to feel like she was perfect and safe to experience love, so she went about her day facing outward, working with all her energy to project a message of high control. She didn't ask for help, didn't risk vulnerability, and she became even more inaccessible to her husband.

Steve's sin was always pleasure of the flesh: drink, sex, money—whatever he could get in the moment. The lack of excess of any one sin kept him from feeling guilty, so he didn't feel he had a "problem." A drink here or there, some pornography on the side, a little flirting at the office. It felt good and no one was getting hurt, so what was the harm? He pinballed up and down from feeling bad about himself to feeling bad about Kelli when he was at home, and then feeling relief when he got a hit of something to release the pressure.

When Sheila walked into his life, she was everything his wife was not. She was free-spirited (wasn't his wife once this way? he hadn't changed, but she had, he thought), open, fun, and best of all, willing to share a bed with him. Instead of an occasional hit, she became a habit, and then Steve and Kelli had all the ingredients for a broken marriage.

That's the point when I met them and we began to talk, the three of us, about how they reached this point. He was shocked and offended when I told him I could predict with stunning accuracy the trajectory of his relationship with Sheila. As wild and sexy as it felt now, with that kind of start, he would just be trading one set of problems for another and, meanwhile, blow up his family, divide his wealth, and carry with him the weight and complication of a failed marriage.

How do you untangle a story like this? The Enemy is very cunning, but he has no new tricks. We can guess what he wants: everyone isolated from each other, prideful they aren't wrong (or at least the other person is more wrong), and unwilling to repent of their sin; they have little to no buckets of forgiveness to offer their partners.

The first step is to anticipate the next attack and movement of the Enemy. How can he get what he wants? How can we identify places where he has set up strongholds? In 2 Corinthians 10:4–5, we read, "For the weapons of our warfare are not carnal, but mighty through God to the pulling down of strong holds; casting down imaginations, and every high thing that exalteth itself against the knowledge of God, and bringing into captivity every thought to the obedience to Christ" (KJV). What exactly is a stronghold? And why is a stronghold important in warfare?

A stronghold is a defensive structure. What does God's Word say about strongholds? "The LORD is a refuge for the oppressed, a stronghold in times of trouble" (Ps. 9:9). In Hebrew it's *misgav*: a cliff or other lofty or inaccessible place; a refuge or a high fort or tower for defense.

> David stayed in the wilderness strongholds and in the hills of the Desert of Ziph. (1 Sam. 23:14)

> [The LORD] is my loving God and my fortress, my stronghold and my deliverer, my shield, in whom I take refuge, who subdues peoples under me. (Ps. 144:2)

> [David] said: "The LORD is my rock, my fortress and my deliverer; my God is my rock, in whom I take refuge, my shield and the horn of my salvation. He is my stronghold, my refuge and my savior—from violent people you save me." (2 Sam. 22:2–3)

Since a stronghold is a place, not a person, it's only a threat if enemies get inside. A spiritual stronghold is *a habitual pattern of thought*, built into one's thought life. And Satan wants to capture people's minds, for the mind is the fortress of the soul, a strategic place where actions follow our thinking. If my mind is convinced pleasure is my pathway to relief, it has a strong "hold" over me. I need to replace this thinking with truth.

> Those who live according to the flesh have their minds set on what the flesh desires; but those who live in accordance with the Spirit have their minds set on what the Spirit desires. The mind governed by the flesh is death, but the mind governed by the Spirit is life and peace. (Rom. 8:5–6)

I don't have to wonder if this is something I struggle with; one look at my calendar, or my search history, or my wallet, or my scale and I will see if I am valuing pleasure over truth. Even when we think we are good at hiding, it literally leaks out of our mouths and signals the world and the watching enemy that we are fair game—come get us. "For the mouth speaks what the heart is full of. A good man brings good things out of the good stored up in him, and an evil man brings evil things out of the evil stored up in him" (Matt. 12:34–35).

Since a stronghold is a way of thinking (and eventually feeling) that has developed in a person over time, there are any number of big feelings that might color our thinking and impact our ability to wage war. Feelings make something seem true, even when it isn't, and once it feels true, it's hard not to identify with it:

> depression (I am depressed)
> unbelief (I am a doubter)
> bad temper (I am a hothead)
> failure (I am a disappointment)
> resentment (I am right)
> worthlessness (I am insignificant)

The lies fill our minds, hold them captive, and keep us from repenting of sin and receiving deliverance.

So how does someone break an enemy hold?

- Confess it by name to minimize its power. Evil loves obscurity, and darkness wants to stay hidden. Ephesians 5:11 urges us to "have nothing to do with the fruitless deeds of darkness, but rather expose them."
- Ask God regularly to reveal dark thoughts. I don't want them to find fertile soil to plant their seeds. I have to wrestle with pride in naming my sin specifically, rather than just saying the generic "forgive me for my sins." I want them exposed to the light and their power broken,

so I press on and name the sinful ways I seek unholy pleasure. "Test me, LORD, and try me, examine my heart and my mind" (Ps. 26:2).

- Ask God to forgive, fighting the urge to justify those thoughts or defend myself. "A broken and contrite heart you, God, will not despise" (Ps. 51:17).

- Finally, replace bad thoughts with good ones, true ones. Reminding myself not to despair, but to have hope; not to accept rejection, but to believe I am a child of God; not to feel fear, but to have peace. It's spiritual exercise, but it keeps me in fighting shape for a war I am constantly engaged in. When I forget this is a war, and I just try to live my life, I lose ground, and untruths seep in.

As I talked to Steve and Kelli about the strongholds they were reinforcing in their own lives and in each other, we all began to repent. Darkness hates repentance; it's one of our most powerful tools to wage battle. When I realize how much God has forgiven me for my incorrect thinking, and just how incorrect it has been, I make room for Him to fill me with hope and restoration. Steve and Kelli have a long journey ahead of them, with plenty of work to do and triggers to disengage. Knowing they're battling not only each other but also an unseen enemy and their own unhealthy thinking has given them a shared mission and a renewed sense that there is a road through this war to victory.

Darkness hates repentance; it's one of our most powerful tools to wage battle.

What matters most to our adversary is getting us to expend energy on ourselves and for ourselves to feel pleasure and distraction. How does he use this striving for his advantage? He lulls me into believing what I want will fix what I *need*. But I can't fix what God wants to heal, and what He wants to heal is my brokenness. Then I am satisfied.

Which pleasures of the flesh most tempt you? What can you do about them?

What strongholds or habitual patterns of thought have held you captive?

What gifts are tempting to love more than the Giver?

Chapter 20

Satan wants me to feel shame.

God redeems me.

"You intended to harm me, but God intended it for good to
accomplish what is now being done, the saving of many lives."
Genesis 50:20

Shame is a disconnector; it isolates us when we most need connection to God
and others. It holds tension in relationships and causes us to hide, for fear if
someone *really knew*, we'd be rejected. Because healing happens in relationship, it's the Enemy's chief goal that we don't act or live in community. He
uses shame as a silencer, and without Christ's intervention, it would be an
effective tactic to prevent attachment to one another and the Lord.

> Little children, you are from God and have overcome them,
> for he who is in you is greater than he who is in the world.
> (1 John 4:4 ESV)

> When he lies, he speaks his native language, for he is a liar
> and the father of lies. (John 8:44)

"Beth, something is going on with Josh's bank account," Todd said with
concern after checking our college son's balance. Josh had been working

three jobs all summer and was saving for his school year. Todd loves a hard worker and was looking to see what had accumulated for Josh's efforts.

"There's nothing there, and he's overdrawn."

Todd went looking for Josh, and a terrible story unfolded. Apparently, Josh was the victim of a convincing phishing scheme. Someone emailed his college address looking for a dog walker. They had pictures and were skilled at deception, so Josh was hooked and naively gave them more information than he should have. As we agreed with the police officer later that day, something appeared too good to be true, and it indeed was. Now all his money was gone.

Josh was crushed—broken, really. Every side job, second job, difficult job he had accepted over the summer resulted in nothing. Every time he had said no to a friend in order to pick up another shift—all the money was gone. On top of that, he felt embarrassed, self-conscious, stupid, angry, ashamed … the list went on.

As we processed the entire event, we asked ourselves, *What was Josh's biggest mistake?* It wasn't answering the ad or even giving his information. His biggest mistake was when something sounded too good to be true, he didn't ask us for counsel. If I had seen the messages going back and forth between him and this potential employer, I would have known with my jaded life view and experiences that it was a scam. But too often, we don't ask for help when we need it.

Todd and I continued to wrestle for days with our parental responsibility in all of it. We waffled between our good American, independent roots ("Some lessons are learned the hard way") and our Spirit-filled identities. We talked about the similarities to when we get in over our heads and are afraid or ashamed to ask the Father for help. What was our goal? How could we use this to give Josh an impression of how God works?

We called Josh into our room and sat him down. He had spent the last two days with a brave face, but we knew it was covering a broken heart. "Josh," Todd began, "I want to let you know your mom and I are going to reimburse you for what was stolen." His head snapped up and he looked at Todd, confused and questioning, yet already somewhat relieved.

Todd continued, "I want you to remember this moment for the rest of your life. I was given what I didn't deserve from my heavenly Father, and I am called to look like Him to you. I want you more than anything to grasp this idea: our Father in heaven delights in giving us back what is lost. He loves you, and in Him, you are not defined by your mistakes." At this point, Todd, Josh, and I were all in tears. It was a holy moment, a redemptive exchange that will pay dividends in Josh's life worth far more than the couple of thousand dollars it cost us.

He loves you, and in Him, you are not defined by your mistakes.

Josh's human nature bit with greed when he was offered a job paying too well for too little work. The Devil didn't make him do that. But when given the opportunity, the Enemy took advantage and entered into Josh's story by wreaking havoc on his hope, his self-image, and his excitement about the future. When it all falls apart, we have a choice. We can sit in the ashes and feel ashamed, or we can submit to God, asking, "How can we use what the Enemy intended to harm me, but instead use it for good?" (see Gen. 50:20). When we involve God, every time He ends up giving us back far more than what we lost.

When I say or do the wrong thing, afterward I tend to replay that event and feel bad, embarrassed, angry, or ashamed. When I replay, I am linking arms with the Enemy, allowing my thoughts to be consumed and wasting time with wrong thinking. When I choose "replay," the Enemy steals from me: time, peace, and relationship. It's okay to reflect on missteps; I can certainly learn from my mistakes. But the better route to take is conviction, which avoids Satan's preference for me to settle into guilt and shame. Here's the difference:

> *Guilt* is something I feel because I have done something bad.
> *Shame* is something I feel because I believe I am bad.
> *Conviction* is the prompting of the Holy Spirit to confess my
> sins. It brings freedom from shame because I realize in God's
> image and by His sacrifice, I am made right in His eyes.

Dr. Curt Thompson, author of *The Soul of Shame*, wrote, "[Shame's] goal is to disintegrate any and every system it targets, be that one's personal story, a family, marriage, friendship, church, school, community, business or political system. Its power lies in its subtlety and its silence, and it will not be satisfied until all hell breaks loose."[11]

Once hell breaks loose, sin flourishes and each sin is like a bullet the Enemy can use over and over again unless confession and sanctification occur. I am convinced Satan reuses his bullets in this war. If I lose my patience with my child, snapping and speaking harsh words, here are all the places carnage can occur:

- I feel bad about how I parented, maybe even guilty or shameful.
- It impacts my next interaction with that child or another one.
- Shame makes me withdraw and I feel like a failure at parenting.
- My child feels belittled and withdraws from family activity.
- My child absorbs a subconscious message that we can talk to those we love without regard.

- My child may confide in his or her friend about our exchange, and consequently, that friend has a negative impression of Christians. It now feels like "us" against "them."
- I retell the story to my husband later in the day, and he feels defensive or judgmental; we divide not over the original issue that upset me but over how I handled it. We fight about how we were fighting.
- Distracted, disconnected, and feeling misunderstood, everything feels worse. That's four people drawn into this mess. The stories could get worse as sin remains unconfessed, resulting in disengagement from community life.

However, if I confess and am sanctified from my sin, then the bullet is instead used for gospel purposes:

- As I vulnerably apologize to my child, I demonstrate humility and open a dialogue on confession.
- Admitting to God that I lost my patience, I am again in awe of how He never does.
- Acknowledging my part in the story affords the opportunity to address the root sin that caused this reaction. Healing can then occur.
- Putting humility on display testifies to God's powerful work in me.

There are catastrophic results to not acknowledging the role shame has in our lives, not the least being broken relationships. I can judge others, and the more I judge, the stronger the presence of shame is in my life. The act of judging others has its origins in our self-judgment. Shamed people shame people.

Satan is relentless in his accusations; he accuses continuously. He hates God and all that God is, which means he hates God's mercy and forgiveness extended to sinful humanity. It doesn't matter what Satan says. "Who will bring any charge against those whom God has chosen? It is God who justifies" (Rom. 8:33). Satan desires to remind believers of our sin and our unworthiness and, in this way, sow doubt into our hearts and minds. God has another way.

Shame wants to disrupt connection between people. Throughout biblical history, shame kept people in broken relationships, stunted their growth, kept them from repentance, from taking risks, and from living all God wanted for them. With an empathetic and attentive listener, I can rewrite the stories of shame I have recorded. The Enemy is more interested in being heard than listening, but being heard actually heals the brain.[12] So I am asking myself how well I listen. How vulnerable am I with people who listen to me? Am I willing to do the work on my own root system and be fertilizer to others?

Shame is powerful, and it's one tactic the Enemy can set into motion where we end up doing the worst damage to ourselves. But I refuse to allow him to have any more mileage from this strategy in my life. I am actively looking for storylines like what happened with Josh where we can flip the script and use what the Enemy intended for evil to tell others of a redemptive God who loves lavishly and without condition.

Where do you see shame creeping into your life? What can you do about it?

What kinds of things do you replay in your mind?

How vulnerable are you with people who listen to you?

Chapter 21

Satan wants me ignorant to the Holy Spirit's power.

God wants to introduce Himself to me.

"God sends angels with special orders to protect you wherever you go, defending you from all harm. If you walk into a trap, they'll be there for you and keep you from stumbling. You'll even walk unharmed among the fiercest powers of darkness, trampling every one of them beneath your feet!"
Psalm 91:11-13 TPT

A friend had given me a book titled *Understanding the Holy Spirit.* To be honest, I was annoyed and a bit prideful, assuming I already understood the Holy Spirit. I knew she was going to ask me if I had read it, so one rare afternoon when Todd had all our young kids out of the house, I took some time for myself to curl up with the book. I opened to the first chapter, which was about prophetic words. Subsequent chapters covered how the Holy Spirit convicts, encourages, and edifies, and how to understand Him, speak with Him, and be filled with Him. I read defensively, assuming my friend was insinuating my relationship with God wasn't all it could be.

In the middle of my reading, our home phone rang, but I decided not to pick it up. It was unique for me to be alone, and I didn't want the interruption.

While it was still ringing, a thought popped in my head: *It's Crist Hamilton on the phone. That's weird*, I thought. *I can't imagine he has our number.*

We were living in Mexico at the time, and not many people had our international home number, certainly not Crist, the father of my sister-in-law. I had never even spoken on the phone with him before. About a minute later, the answering machine kicked on and the caller left a message. "Beth and Todd, it's Crist Hamilton. I was hoping to catch you …"

My mouth hung open. *Really, Lord?* I repented of my unbelief and told the Lord His stunt had worked. I would stop putting Him in a box that felt familiar and controllable and start wondering what else He could do.

Today, God has increased my understanding of many of the tools He has placed in my toolbox. When I am not able to see what God can, He prompts me to response or prayer through prophetic words or thoughts He places in my mind. Or He nudges me to reach out to someone—sometimes even a stranger. Today in church I felt prompted to pray for the man in front of me. I told him I was seeing in my mind a giant *X*, which after sitting with it a minute, felt like a symbol of multiplication. I prayed God would multiply this man's kingdom impact, and he shared that he and his wife had just adopted two children.

Recently, I had a phone call with someone I had never met, a powerful music producer with whom I have a mutual friend. We were discussing the potential for us to collaborate on a project he was working on, tying together an artist's heart for orphans with his platform in Latin America. As I hung up, I told my assistant, "I doubt that will go anywhere. I've had dozens of those calls and most end up just being good ideas." I was ready to move on to the next thing, when God stopped me with a thought I knew I hadn't authored (that's what prophetic words sound like). *Introduce him to Samuel.*

I hadn't paused to pray after the call and ask God what He was up to; I was just ready to cross it off my list and move on. I confess this because sometimes we expect that if we want God to speak to us, we need to have fasted that day or be in a meditative posture with our foreheads scrunched up in earnest prayer. It doesn't always happen that way; for me, most of the time, God speaks to me when I am moving too fast and He wants me to slow down so I can obey.

Samuel is a family friend, the son of my Mexican pastor, and a talented musician. He didn't make a living with music and hadn't done anything professionally; he was just genuinely talented. I called the mutual friend I had with the music producer and told him I wanted to introduce Samuel to the producer. He hesitated and said, "Beth, if I had a dollar for every person who wanted to send him a video of their child, niece, neighbor, etc.… The truth is you don't have the relational capital to do that, and if I do it, I would be using mine and I just used some of it simply to introduce him to you."

I told him I understood; I was just trying to be obedient to the Lord. "How about this?" I continued. "I will send you a video of him singing. If you like it, you pass it along. If you don't, then no worries; I did what I could."

An hour later, the producer called me and asked if I could set up a meeting—and today, Samuel Adrian is a recording artist, signed soon after to the producer's label. God moves in ways we don't understand and sometimes don't even believe. His Spirit wants to encourage us, challenge us, warn us … and the more we understand the spiritual realm, the more effective gospel bearers we will be.

One of my favorite biblical examples of someone who understood God's power comes from 1 Kings 18. It's the story of Elijah and his showdown against the Baal god during a severe famine in Samaria. The prophet Elijah confronted Israel's King Ahab, who was married to Jezebel—lover of other gods. "I have not made trouble for Israel," Elijah told him. "But you and your father's family have. You have abandoned the LORD's commands and have followed the Baals" (v. 18).

God loves *chutzpah*, that utter audacity. He responds to it, and Elijah had plenty of it, telling Ahab (who was the king!) that *he* was the problem.

He went on to challenge him to bring 450 Baal prophets and 400 Asherah prophets for a showdown. "Elijah went before the people and said, 'How long will you waver between two opinions? If the LORD is God, follow him; but if Baal is God, follow him'" (v. 21).

When he asked, "How long will you waver?" the word is *pacach* in Hebrew, meaning "to hop, to hesitate, to dance." God has power and wants to use us to demonstrate it, but too often I can dance back and forth like the watching Israelites and waver between two opinions. God is asking me to believe and follow. The people said nothing, and Elijah instructed them to get two bulls. They would build an altar for theirs and he would for his, and "the god who answers by fire—he is God" (v. 24).

"At noon Elijah began to taunt them. 'Shout louder!' he said. 'Surely he is a god! Perhaps he is deep in thought, or busy, or traveling. Maybe he is sleeping and must be awakened'" (v. 27). Elijah was so confident in the available power of God, he was trash-talking the Baal prophets. When he asked if their god was "busy," in Hebrew it literally means "going to the bathroom."

Nothing happened. Elijah then called to the people to come to him, and he repaired the Lord's altar in front of them, which had been torn down, and dug a trench around it. Then he said to them, "Fill four large jars with water and pour it on the offering and on the wood" (v. 33).

Where did the water come from? Too far to hike from the Mediterranean, and in a drought, it would have had to come from their own water supply, allowing the people to take part in this incredible miracle. God has always had a heart for us to participate in His miracles. He was asking these drought sufferers to put their chips all in, to not waver or doubt any longer, and to give the last and rest of what they had. I see Him challenge me in the same way: step out, risk, speak up, sacrifice first … and then the power flows. God loves involving us! He wants our faith to grow, and one of the greatest ways it does is through our generosity and boldness. I may have only a few drops in my "canteen," but if God asks for it, I need to give it. There's no outgiving God.

"Do it again," he said, and they did it again.

"Do it a third time," he ordered, and they did it the third time. The water ran down around the altar and even filled the trench.

At the time of sacrifice, the prophet Elijah stepped forward and prayed: "LORD, the God of Abraham, Isaac and Israel, let it be known today that you are God in Israel and that I am your servant and have done all these things at your command. Answer me, LORD, answer me, so these people will know that you, LORD, are God, and that you are turning their hearts back again."

Then the fire of the LORD fell and burned up the sacrifice, the wood, the stones and the soil, and also licked up the water in the trench.

When all the people saw this, they fell prostrate and cried, "The LORD—he is God! The LORD—he is God!" (vv. 34–39)

God loves involving us! He wants our faith to grow, and one of the greatest ways it does is through our generosity and boldness.

God regularly uses the least likely—and does it when the odds are stacked against them. That's always been His way. I don't like the subtle undertones in some church settings that there are some who are more powerful—better—than others. God has empowered His people from their first faith steps onward. From the very beginning, it isn't dependent on what we bring to the table but on what God has already done. We don't earn God's power; we are vessels of it. And the more we pour ourselves out, the more He fills us up. I love imagining the fit the Enemy threw when the fire fell from heaven at Elijah's call. Satan had been stirring up compromise, discouragement, fear, and had more people on his side than those demonstrating faithfulness, but God only needed *one* to display His power.

Some people laugh when I give God credit for seemingly trivial things—like on-time deliveries and good weather, as if it wasn't God—but I think the opposite. I imagine He does a lot more than I am aware of. I can get into my day, operating on my own strength, using my own reason and resources, and at some point, I become sloppy or worn out. But God never does; He's ever-present, picking up the pieces and guiding, putting on display His power and protection. I can be oblivious to the Enemy's tricks, and he loves that, so he can slink around without my fighting him off. But I can be equally oblivious to God's working, and that's just as dangerous. I am working on the throughout-the-day kind of conversation God designed us to have with Him: where I tell Him here's all the water in my canteen, or I feel outnumbered, or I would love You to show off right now, or like Elijah in the next chapter (1 Kings 19), I confess my fatigue.

The Passion Translation of Psalm 91 reminds me of His constant presence amid the war we are in:

When we live our lives within the shadow of God Most High,
	our secret hiding place, we will always be shielded from
		harm.
	How then could evil prevail against us or disease infect us?
God sends angels with special orders to protect you wherever
	you go,
	defending you from all harm.
If you walk into a trap, they'll be there for you
	and keep you from stumbling.
You'll even walk unharmed among the fiercest powers of
	darkness,
	trampling every one of them beneath your feet!
For here is what the Lord has spoken to me:
	"Because you have delighted in me as my great lover,
	I will greatly protect you.
	I will set you in a high place, safe and secure before my face.
	I will answer your cry for help every time you pray,
	and you will find and feel my presence
	even in your time of pressure and trouble.
	I will be your glorious hero and give you a feast." (vv. 9–15)

When the Spirit allows us to see His power demonstrated, He is acting as our glorious hero. I am at my best when I remember only He saves, and only He is who I should call. Sometimes that demonstration is jaw-dropping, like a healing or a miracle. But most of the time He moves in ways we don't understand or appreciate until we look up.

What do you believe about prophetic thoughts and how God uses them?

When have you seen God respond to your *chutzpah*?

What has God invited you to participate in? Is He inviting you now?

Chapter 22

Satan wants to mess with my body. God intervenes.

"Is anyone among you sick? Let them call the elders of the church to pray over them and anoint them with oil in the name of the Lord."
James 5:14

In March, we spent a weekend in Texas enjoying some family fellowship and Texas hospitality. It should have been the perfect weekend, but as I walked along San Antonio's famed River Walk, all I could think was *Where is the closest bathroom?* I'd been battling a stomach flu for a week, and I was tired of it. A month later, I left in the middle of our church's Easter service because my stomach was upset again.

May and June were a blur, but we eventually consulted a doctor. Why couldn't I keep food down anymore? I'd never been sick as an adult; I'd never even had allergies. By July, the doctors had a diagnosis: gastroparesis, a condition in which your food doesn't digest, so after an extended time in your stomach, it has to come back up. But there was no reason for me to have developed this condition. Most people who have it are diabetic, have had intestinal surgery, or have some sort of tumor or blockage. Also, the doctors added, "this condition usually gets progressively worse and has no cure."

On the last day of July, José Angel, a pastor friend of ours, came to our house in Mexico. Although he looks like he forgets to get ready each morning, he has a heart of pure gold. I have trouble admitting weakness, and I don't like to ask for help, so I hadn't told Pastor José Angel about the extent of my illness. In fact, he didn't even know it was my stomach that had been the problem. All he knew was I hadn't been coming around his ministry—which made his following comment to me even more amazing.

"Beth, I had a dream last week, and I'm sorry it has taken this long to tell you about it. I know you've been sick, but I want you to know God has healed you." My conservative roots kicked in, and I lifted an eyebrow in skepticism. José Angel continued, "In my dream, there was a demon wrapped around your stomach, but it has now been released. God has allowed it for a season, so when you encounter demonic forces in the future, you'll recognize them and how they move. He wants to use you to free others. But today you are free, so go and walk in your healing." He finished and smiled.

Not one thing in his entire story seemed believable to me; still, I let him pray over me. Disappointed, I felt no "tingling" of miraculous healing. I walked back to the house, immediately got sick, and felt frustrated. Late one night two days later, my friend Sonia, who's married to another pastor in Mexico, called me on the phone. She sounded anxious. "Beth, I just had this dream about you and had to call and tell you about it …" She proceeded to describe the same dream Pastor José Angel had—same message, same promise of healing. The odd thing: Pastor José Angel and Sonia didn't even know each other.

Now God had my attention.

I scheduled a trip home to Ohio the next week, where I planned to see a medical specialist to pursue further treatment. I wrestled with what to tell him. I wasn't even sure what to think myself. In his office, I said, "Here's my file, here are my tests, here's my health history—and here's my frustration with the last couple of months." I probably told him far more than he needed to know. He nodded, looked over the files, and eventually concluded, "You're very sick."

I looked away. *Should I tell him about the dreams?*

I dove in. "Here's the thing. For the past week, I have been feeling better. Not all at once or anything, but a little better every day. I've been eating some, and it's been staying down. I don't know how you feel about this—I don't really know how I feel about it—but I think a demon may have been released and I am healed."

"Wow." He paused. "Normally, since these tests are less than a month old, I would use them to determine my treatment plan, but let's repeat them and see where we stand." That seemed logical and safe. I liked what I could read on a chart. We repeated the myriad of tests.

Days later, the specialist called me. "Beth, in my left hand are the test results you brought from Mexico showing me you are very sick. But in my right hand are the tests you took a few days ago telling me you are healthy. I propose no ongoing medical treatment for you at this time." He paused, then added, "And yes, I do think it's a miracle."[13]

I don't understand it, but I need to testify to it. Do I think a demon was wrapped around my stomach? I don't know, but it sure felt like it. My faith grew throughout this process. It grew when I let José Angel pray over me. It grew again when I let Sonia pray over me. It grew when I boldly told the doctor in Ohio about my friends' dreams. And it grew as I heard the new results and rejoiced in my miraculous healing.

If faith could fit in a frame the way a painting does, then we might get tired of looking at it after a couple of years. But faith, as it grows, keeps demanding a new and larger frame to be displayed in. I think the Lord loves to do things that are unexpected—things beyond what we can control or predict. It forces our canvas of faith to get bigger. God consistently breaks the boundaries (my frame) with which I've surrounded Him. Enlarging the frame of my faith means admitting my finiteness and rigidity. It means He is dangerously greater than I can define or even understand.

Faith, as it grows, keeps
demanding a new and larger
frame to be displayed in.

I am different now: I minister differently, I pray differently, I look for new aspects of His character. I no longer say "never" because I have had an up-close and personal encounter with a demon. I now think literally anything is possible. People can reconcile, bodies can heal, doors can open. I don't know why or how or when, but I know we can hope, and I know we can believe. I also know we are opposed, and there is a whole world of warfare we only understand in part.

Some people would look at José Angel and think about all the ways they could "teach and train" him. But I'm not sure I can ever match what he offered to me. He and Sonia were listening to the Lord so intently they caught a message meant for me. Then they trusted in the Spirit that led them to share what must have been uncomfortable. And their act of faith helped heal me and increased my own faith.

Since then, when I hear of someone's physical ailments, I have often wondered how much of it could be spiritual. I have now on occasion had the courage to ask someone if I could pray to that end, and sometimes, I will testify, I have seen healings—headaches and dizzy spells that did end up being more spiritual than physical. Other times, it seems like there is an infection, or a root cause for illness, that is more a result of living in a broken world. *How do we pray? How do we know the difference? When is it spiritual and when is it simply medical?*

It's *always* spiritual. Even if the Enemy didn't cause someone to become ill, he will use it. We can pray toward a spiritual relief for anyone we encounter who is physically hurting. How God answers, when He answers, that's not for me to measure. I know He doesn't like it when we are sick, because He promises one day "'He will wipe every tear from their eyes. There will be no more death,' or mourning or crying or pain, for the old order of things has passed away" (Rev. 21:4).

Jesus healed a woman who could not straighten herself. He said in Luke 13:16, "Then should not this woman, a daughter of Abraham, *whom Satan has kept bound for eighteen long years*, be set free on the Sabbath day from what bound her?" Jesus confirmed for us right there that Satan messes with our bodies. Later, in Acts 10:38, we read: "how God anointed Jesus of Nazareth with the Holy Spirit and power, and how he went around doing good and *healing all who were under the power of the devil*, because God was with him." Spiritual forces are at work against us, so to consider prayer over a hurting body with that in mind is always appropriate.

The Enemy wants to mess with our bodies, because at the very least, it requires energy from us we now can't spend elsewhere. He also wants to mess with our bodies because it messes with our heads; we get confused and discouraged. Does it seem like we see patterns of enemy attack on a person or a family physically? Yes. I wish it wasn't so, but we have all seen it—sometimes it feels like a person or a family just can't catch a break. I am committing to bolder prayer intervention for those I love who fall ill—for binding the Enemy in the name of Jesus and asking God for complete healing. We have authority as co-heirs with Christ, and He tells us to use it.

How has God grown your spiritual frame?

How have you seen the Enemy mess with the body?

When can you ask God to intervene and heal?

Chapter 23

Satan wants me self-absorbed.

God says, "Others first."

"We know that we are of God, and the whole world
is under the sway of the evil one."
1 John 5:19 CSB

When I was a young missionary, before I had any children, I was making lunch for a visiting high school youth group. They were all crowded around a kitchen island, and it was as if I were a short-order cook with all their requests.

"I don't do crunchy peanut butter."

"I only like white bread."

"Does the jelly have chunks in it?"

"Can I have the organic peanut butter?"

I stood there thinking (the way you do before you have children), *When my children grow up, they are going to eat any combination of PB&J anyone offers, anywhere!*

With that goal in mind, as our family began and grew, I eventually bought wheat bread one week and white the next. I switched between smooth and crunchy peanut butter, and grape jelly, strawberry jelly, and sometimes *no* jelly. I was determined that if my children came to your house, they would eat PB&J however you served it to them. I know that sounds silly—it's just sandwiches—but when we start with the end goal in mind and reverse engineer our choices accordingly, we are more likely to hit our mark.

It works with the larger questions too. Who do I want to *be* at the end of my life? I want to be standing strong, committed to community, and fully immovable in my faith. I want to know that when the Devil comes my way, he finds a formidable match.

This means I have to fight my own selfish nature to be independent and judgmental when circumstances of life are threatening or uncomfortable. I am just as tempted as anyone else to be lazy or self-seeking. It's not easy to think of others first, but it's absolutely our calling.

All over the New Testament, God gave instructions for how His kids should act toward others:

> *Love one another, give preference to one another, honor one another, be of the same mind toward one another, do not judge one another, build one another up, accept one another, greet one another with a holy kiss, care for one another, serve one another, bear one another's burdens, show tolerance for one another, be kind to one another, do not lie to one another, comfort one another, encourage one another, spur one another on toward love and good deeds, do not complain about one another, confess your sins to one another, pray for one another, be hospitable to one another, clothe yourself with humility toward one another, have fellowship with one another . . .* (and that's not even all of them!)

God knows when we act lovingly, we put our supernatural nature on display. We are announcing: I don't belong here; I have been redeemed. Don't mess with me, Satan; I come with Holy Spirit power. I am not easy pickings. God also knew this would be a spiritual battle to love one another, with evil and temptation discrediting us at every turn. Since roughly one-quarter of everything Jesus said had to do with spiritual battles, it's safe to assume He saw our understanding of the war swirling around us as mission critical.

It turns out one of the biggest tools we have in our spiritual tool belts to fight against the Enemy is a spiritual family. "Do you not know that you are a temple of God and that the Spirit of God dwells in you?" (1 Cor. 3:16 NASB). "You" in the original text is plural, meaning "Don't you know that *all you all* are a temple of God …?" Our spiritual family reminds us of who we are and cheers us on when we forget the dream of looking like a piece of heaven here on earth.

> It turns out one of the biggest tools we have in our spiritual tool belts to fight against the Enemy is a spiritual family.

One of my favorite stories from history is of Mahalia Jackson. She was a gospel singer and a dear friend of Martin Luther King Jr. There are accounts of him traveling and feeling overwhelmed, and he would call and ask her to sing to encourage him. The night before he delivered the "I have a dream" speech, he gathered with his closest circle and shared with them that he was struggling with the decision to use a metaphor in his speech about either America's bad check ("promises it can't cash") or the idea of having a dream.

In the end, he decided to talk about the bad check, and on August 28, 1963, in front of 250,000 people, he started out, "In a sense we've come to our nation's capital to cash a check. When the architects of our republic wrote the magnificent words of the Constitution and the Declaration of Independence, they were signing a promissory note to which every American was to fall heir."

Then Mahalia leaned over almost ten minutes into it (she was on the podium with him) and yelled to her friend, "Tell them about the dream, Martin!"[14] He pushed his notes over to the left corner of his lectern and stated boldly, "I have a dream that one day this nation will rise up.... I have a dream that one day every valley shall be exalted, every hill and mountain shall be made low, the rough places will be made plain, and the crooked places will be made straight, and the glory of the Lord shall be revealed, and all flesh shall see it together."[15] He was quoting powerful words from the prophet Isaiah.

I want to acknowledge the problem: we have an enemy who is attacking both God's kids and those who have yet to know Him as their Father. We have vulnerable children, struggling adults, hurting families, and evil running rampant. But I want to say (thanks, Mahalia!) *there is a dream*—a spiritual dream—that lost children come to the Father, that people experience healing, that evil strongholds are demolished, and community is experienced.

"We know that we are of God, and the whole world is under the sway of the evil one" (1 John 5:19 CSB). The definition of "sway" is "rule" or "control." There is a clear distinction between those of us under the control of God and those who are left (and by default not yet rescued from) under the sway or control of the Enemy. It's time I see my spiritual siblings as the gifts they are and do all I can to serve them and build them up. It's also time I see those not in God's family as desperately lost and do all I can to serve them and build them up. There is no time for self-absorption. God made it abundantly clear through His example and then His Word: be about the Body and the lost.

As a spiritual family, many subjects can divide and distract us: Do we raise our hands or not? Drink alcohol or not? How do we feel about the Holy Spirit and His gifts? Who do we vote for? How do we feel about women in leadership? Divorce? Racial issues? Baptism? Tithing? Bible translations? The combination of sin plus enemy attack on the Bride has caused pain to the Church ever since it was born. We can be sure that in this world, we have an enemy and he wants us focused on our fears, divided against ourselves, and angry with one another.

Paul wrote to the church in Rome about the issues dividing them. It wasn't about hands raised or sprinkling versus dunking. For them, it was food, Sabbath, circumcision, all issues of the law. There were Jews who had been following the law a long time, and Gentiles who didn't even know the law. They were commingling and feeling judgmental of the "other." They hid it well behind well-articulated arguments of theology, but it was a thinly veiled display of self-absorption. They might as well have said, "This is about me, what I think, what I believe is true, how I want to live and practice my faith ..." Paul wasn't having it, mainly because it was impacting their heaven-on-earth mission, and so he said quite a bit to them in a letter recorded in Romans 14:

> Accept the one whose faith is weak, without quarreling over disputable matters. One person's faith allows them to eat anything, but another, whose faith is weak, eats only vegetables. The one who eats everything must not treat with contempt the one who does not, and the one who does not eat everything must not judge the one who does, for God has accepted them. Who are you to judge someone else's servant? To their own master, servants stand or fall. And they will stand, for the Lord is able to make them stand.
>
> One person considers one day more sacred than another; another considers every day alike. Each of them should be fully convinced in their own mind. Whoever regards one

day as special does so to the Lord. Whoever eats meat does so to the Lord, for they give thanks to God; and whoever abstains does so to the Lord and gives thanks to God. For none of us lives for ourselves alone, and none of us dies for ourselves alone. If we live, we live for the Lord; and if we die, we die for the Lord. So, whether we live or die, we belong to the Lord....

You, then, why do you judge your brother or sister? Or why do you treat them with contempt? For we will all stand before God's judgment seat....

Therefore let us stop passing judgment on one another. Instead, make up your mind not to put any stumbling block or obstacle in the way of a brother or sister....

Let us therefore make every effort to do what leads to peace and to mutual edification. Do not destroy the work of God for the sake of food. All food is clean, but it is wrong for a person to eat anything that causes someone else to stumble. It is better not to eat meat or drink wine or to do anything else that will cause your brother or sister to fall.

So whatever you believe about these things keep between yourself and God. Blessed is the one who does not condemn himself by what he approves. (vv. 1–8, 10, 13, 19–22)

Paul was writing to a church with sincerely held differences (which is absolutely okay), with varying levels of knowledge (which is expected in a church), and with different degrees of conscience sensitivity. He was encouraging them to strive for oneness in Christ over insisting on being right or heard.[16] This is the end we are to keep in mind. Becoming one in Christ means letting go of personal agendas and selfish ambitions. The cause of Jesus and the worth of a soul must be the most important things.

For the Romans, as well as for us today, Paul's point is the same: in "matters of conscience" (i.e., personal convictions concerning practices that are neither ordered nor forbidden in the Bible), Christians are to follow two standards: refrain from judging or condemning other kids of God whose opinions differ from your own (14:1–12), and refrain from using your freedom in ways that pressure or encourage another believer to sin by going against his or her own conscience (vv. 13–23).

The bottom line for Paul was love. As he had already said in Romans 13:8, "Owe nothing to anyone except to love one another; for the one who loves his neighbor has fulfilled the Law" (NASB). Romans 14 explains how Christians can fulfill the law of love even when they disagree, which we inevitably will!

There are some gray areas in life. Can we live peaceably with one another—not violating our own conscience, but making it a matter between us and the Lord, not between us and each other? On a scale of one to ten, the cross is a ten. Love is a ten. If someone returns your email with nuanced language that you don't appreciate: not a ten. If someone lets their kids watch a movie you don't agree with: not a ten. Paul used his letter to say as practically as he could, *Whatever you are feeling passionate about, make sure Jesus said it was important. If it's just tradition or opinion, don't let it divide.*

God's family isn't perfect and churches aren't perfect places, but it's our privilege to serve and protect, even at our own expense. This is where the Enemy's strategy of self-absorption comes into play. Let's start from a place of loving the Bride of Christ and not approaching it like a Yelp review. The judging, rating, reviewing, "liking" culture cannot permeate the Church and our faith communities.

God says love.

The Enemy says find something wrong with the Church or its people or its leaders. If we can see what's wrong there, then it's a short step to pointing our fingers at God. We are so used to rating our products and our restaurant experiences, we can be tempted to judge one another. But God says, I am the only one who can judge, and even *I* won't do it.

Loving others and honoring God take precedence over everything. The Great Commission and the Great Commandment can carry us a long way. The Great Commission says to go out into the world—not to judge it, not to join it, but to share with it the good news of Jesus Christ. The Great Commandment says to love them, at great cost to yourself, all the time and unconditionally—the way He loves us. God's family has an opportunity to model love that places the interests of others above self.

In Hebrew, the phrase *tikkun olam* means "to repair the world, to make straight, establish or repair." God's design is to use us, created in His image, to act as His ambassadors in this world, to literally make straight what is crooked. There are plenty of famous examples of history-making repairers of the world, like Mother Teresa and George Müller, but my most recent favorite is a Polish pediatrician and children's book author named Dr. Janusz Korczak. In 1912, he started Orphan Society, a place where orphaned and vulnerable children lived in community. He was trying out models of family-based care and was way ahead of his time in understanding that children should not be warehoused but function best in a family context.

When Poland was occupied in 1939, and the Nazis moved all the Jews into the ghetto, he chose to live with the orphans. On August 5, 1942, twelve staff, two hundred children, and Dr. Korczak were taken to a concentration camp. The story goes that he asked the children to bring their favorite toys or books for the journey and to dress up. He knew where they were headed, but he wanted to spare them the terror of their coming fate. When they arrived at the gate of the concentration camp, one of the guards recognized him as his child's favorite author and offered to spare his life if he would just help get the children inside. He said to the guard as he headed through the gates, "You don't leave a child in distress."[17]

Dr. Korczak was modeling God's heart. God will never leave us in distress. He is with us and will go into the darkest corners of the earth. The world is decaying, humanity is destroying itself, there is pain and death and all kinds of other confusing expressions of evil, but God will not leave us. And He is asking us to do the same: don't leave the lost, the least of these, in distress. Reach out, spend yourself on others. Love one another; sacrifice for one another. Ask Him to speak to you, to lead you; say yes to any special assignment. Die to self. Be humble. Serve one another.

When the Enemy can keep us worried and absorbed in our own universes, not looking around at others, then the lights inside of us can't shine and attract those in darkness. I can be a Christ follower and still be fixated on my own pain and my own agenda. Even the endless need to express my opinions on social media, or in debates, or within my family can work against a spiritual agenda, which was always designed with us as listeners (James would tell us to be slow to speak). Showing and saying where and how I have it all figured out sounds like a good idea, but in truth, it turns me inward, and life as one of God's kids is best lived with an outward focus on the needs of my spiritual family.

Who do I want to *be* at the end of my life?

Who cheers you on and points out when you are being self-absorbed?

What have you seen divide God's family?

How have you seen service to others form community?

Chapter 24

Satan wants me to build my own kingdom.

God is the chief architect.

"Store up for yourselves treasures in heaven, where moths and vermin do not destroy, and where thieves do not break in and steal. For where your treasure is, there your heart will be also."
Matthew 6:20-21

I once visited the ancient town of Laodicea. It is located in modern-day Turkey and geographically situated halfway between two first-century towns, Hierapolis and Colossae. Celebrated for being the "Spa of the East," Hierapolis is known for its hot mineral springs that heat up to 120 degrees. I enjoyed trying out the waters and recreating there with friends. Seen as a holy city, it attracted people for the healing properties attributed to the hot springs. Over on the other side of Laodicea, but higher in elevation, was the town Colossae—famous for its cool mountain springs where travelers would stop for refreshment.

Laodicea was a place of fancy people and plenty of wealth. It's where the mint was located and they had a coin in circulation that said, "We did it ourselves." They were referencing the rebuilding of their town after several devastating earthquakes when they didn't accept Roman government aid. Most towns asked Rome for financial help in reconstruction, but not Laodicea; they were proud of their self-sufficiency.

God would write Laodicea an often-misunderstood message in Revelation 3:14–16, "To the angel of the church in Laodicea write: These are the words of the Amen, the faithful and true witness, the ruler of God's creation. I know your deeds, that you are neither cold nor hot. I wish you were either one or the other! So, because you are lukewarm—neither hot nor cold—I am about to spit you out of my mouth."

How many times in a youth group setting did I hear something along the lines of either be for God or against Him, but don't sit in the middle. This isn't what He meant at all. The water that ran together in Laodicea was neither hot and healing (like in Hierapolis) nor cold and refreshing (like in Colossae), but a mingling of both the neighboring towns. It was a sore point for them, having plenty of money and still terrible water. God was exposing this bruise as He wrote those words. When He said either be hot or cold, He wasn't saying be for Me or against Me (He doesn't want anyone to be against Him!). He was saying *be for something*! Use what you have to build the church—either be healing or be refreshing, but don't be nothing! Lukewarm water was good for nothing. *You've lost your mission, Laodicea, and you make Me sick—be known for something!* God wanted them to build rather than hold on to the stones—to use what they have been given to further a heavenly agenda over a personal one. Matthew says it like this: "Do not store up for yourselves treasures on earth, where moths and vermin destroy, and where thieves break in and steal. But store up for yourselves treasures in heaven, where moths and vermin do not destroy, and where thieves do not break in and steal. For where your treasure is, there your heart will be also" (6:19–21).

The same message is true for me today. When I was in Israel the first time in 2010, our guide, Ray Vander Laan, was teaching on the biblical character David. Before he was a king, David was a shepherd, and to protect his flock, he would've carried a handful of stones to throw at whatever might threaten his animals. And when a giant came to threaten his people, he couldn't pretend to know how to use the military equipment; he used what was familiar: stones. Ray challenged us to consider what we do naturally all the time and to ask God how He might use it. What can we be known for and offer as a kingdom resource?

This enemy is a threat to us, in the same sense Goliath once was. Taunting, intimidating, aggressive, the giant was defeated when God's kid used what he knew in battle. When I think about the stone I can throw, I inventory the gifts, abilities, resources, experiences, and tools in my hand I can raise against our enemy. Anyone can do it; in fact, David's story teaches us even children can face this threat and win. Psalm 8:2 says, "Through the praise of children and infants you have established a stronghold against your enemies, to silence the foe and the avenger." Worship is a stone we have to throw, a weapon against our ever-present enemy.

What would happen if we all used the influence we have, the natural abilities, the hard-earned capacities and came together and threw our stones against this giant? I want to see Laodicea as a cautionary tale, of people who became full of themselves and their own abilities, and while they looked rich, they spent themselves on themselves. God found that sickening and challenged them and me every time I read it to be known for using what He's given for kingdom advancement and enemy defeat.

Early in my missionary story, a guest, Mike, traveled with us to a mountain orphanage several hours away. We stopped by a grocery store on our way there, wanting to bring resources and provision that were difficult for them to procure. We split up in the store, Todd, Mike, and I, each with assignments to gather different items. When we met at the checkout, Mike had some meat products and I told him to put them back because the orphanage didn't have refrigeration.

"Well, then, we are in the *wrong* store," he told me.

We made a second stop at an appliance store and checked out the selection of refrigerators. They were lined up in order of expense, and I found myself looking at the base models that were smaller, cost effective, and sufficient for their needs. Mike was at the other end of the row, looking at the biggest, most expensive options.

"Mike, they have never had a refrigerator. This one is more than fine," I said, pointing to an economical choice. "They will just be grateful …" My voice trailed off as he came barreling at me and I could tell I was about to be on the receiving end of his strong opinion.

"Beth," he said loudly, looking at me with conviction, "always remember this: when you give gifts in the name of Jesus, *you give brass ring, not baseline.*"

When you give gifts in the name of Jesus, you give brass ring, not baseline.

And just like that, his choice word landed. Proverbs 25:11 says, "Timely advice is lovely, like golden apples in a silver basket" (NLT). I have never served the same since. It's God's way to give the best, to share generously, to be known for how we offer. It paves the way for the gospel. It requires fighting the temptation to think only about myself—fighting against being a stone holder versus a stone thrower.

Jesus, teach me to give away what You've given to me, to face giants, and to be known for how I fight. Help me to use all You've given to me (gifts, trials, lessons, resources, time, blessings) for Your purpose and glory. Spiritual five-alarm fires are going on all around me—people hurting, calamity, and crisis everywhere. May we be spiritual firefighters, running to the needs, unafraid of threatening darkness.

What are you known for?

What stone can you throw?

When have you settled on giving baseline? What can you do about it now?

Part III

Standing Strong

"Be steadfast, immovable, always abounding in the work of the Lord."
1 Corinthians 15:58 ESV

Chapter 25

God is sovereign over Satan.

"Simon, Simon, Satan has asked to sift all of you as wheat."
Luke 22:31

I was feeling tired. It had been a long week with many demands, and I wasn't sleeping well. I was *over-functioning* as an adult—over-parenting, over-working, over-friending—working to prove I could do it all, and that perfect storm made me vulnerable for the Enemy to come in and effectively whisper to me I was failing, or something was going to drop, or I was not good enough.

The week worsened: a child in a fender bender, a colleague misunderstanding, a headache I couldn't shake, computer problems, disconnections with Todd; it felt like I was swimming against the stream. Worse, my "window of tolerance" (the ability to manage setbacks and disappointment) was shrinking, and what should have been blips became speed bumps. I went to the doctor for a routine visit and learned one more piece of bad news: my normally stellar heart rate was out of control and requiring medication.

"You need to make some changes," the doctor said.

I drove away from his office, rushing to a meeting I was both late for and responsible for. My car made an obnoxious beeping noise and the dashboard read, "Speed exceeds limit." A crash was coming; all the signs were pointing to it. What makes me do too much, drive too fast, try to balance all the plates myself? The sense I need to obey feelings instead of heeding wisdom. But the solution isn't only cutting out things or slowing down. It all starts in my mind, where I need to settle and remind myself: God is sovereign, and saving and solving are His departments, not mine.

God is sovereign, and saving and solving are His departments, not mine.

Paul wrote that we are to take "captive every thought" (2 Cor. 10:5), we are to "set [our] minds on things above" (Col. 3:2), and we are to renew our minds (Rom. 12:2). Repeatedly, he reinforced that spiritual work is to first be worked out in our heads, and then our feelings will follow. I get myself in trouble when I rely on feelings as a thermometer for my spiritual health or my to-do list. If I only spiritually engaged in this war when I *felt* like it, I wouldn't be much of a warrior.

Psalm 94:18–19 says, "When I said, 'My foot is slipping,' your unfailing love, LORD, supported me. When anxiety was great within me, your consolation brought me joy." "Supported" in the Hebrew is *yisadeni*, defined as "held up, propped, supported, sustained, stayed, held," and is a metaphor taken from anything falling that is then shored up or buttressed. My foot was slipping, and a hard fall was ahead of me, whether I invited it or it found me. Unbelievably, God tells us how to live and how to trust, and when we don't listen and follow, He is still there to buttress us. We can either fight it or allow His hand to support us through the difficult circumstances and seasons.

I was leading an important task force at work and decided to sit down with a piece of paper and imagine all the ways the Enemy would try to disrupt us. I listed the potential for miscommunication and division in decisions. I prayed about the process and the people involved. Then one of the key members, whom I wholeheartedly appreciate, said something I wish he hadn't (which today seems like no big deal), and I became frustrated with him. I called to let him know how I was feeling and hung up feeling worse. Then it hit me: Satan overplayed his hand. This wasn't about him or me. Sure, we partnered with the Enemy (he spoke out of turn and I didn't give the benefit of the doubt), but Satan took the bat we handed him and hit us over the head with it. I played right into it.

Realizing this was spiritual warfare, I knew I needed to spiritually battle my way through it. After first confessing my sin to God, I called my colleague back and did what my Bible tells me: I extended him grace. I said let's fight side by side instead of face to face. What does the Enemy want? A divided leadership, resentful team, chaos ... We agreed to stick together, overcommunicate, and pray toward a Spirit-filled conclusion.

And the Shepherd won. When I remember I am the sheep, so needy of His guidance, I avoid the dangers of the wild. When I insist like a stubborn goat that I know best, I end up taking far too many steps and get lost along the way. God reminds me in the familiar and powerful passage of Psalm 23 that all I need, He will provide—both in moments of activity and in moments of rest. He is with me when I have everything I need and when I am square in the presence of my enemy.

From Psalm 23:

> The LORD is my shepherd, I lack nothing.
> He makes me lie down in green pastures, (vv. 1–2a)

The first thing He does as my Shepherd is ask me to lie down, to rest. We live in a restless culture, and the question is: How can I be a nonanxious presence in a hurried world? Anxiety comes from feeling like I don't have and am not enough, and this makes me feel unsafe. What did David actually mean when he said, "I lack nothing"?

It reminds me of a time when I saw sheep grazing in Israel. It wasn't in a field full of waist-high alfalfa (the way my mind imagines it as I read this verse). It was on a rocky hillside, where the sheep rely on the shepherd for guidance to the bits of grass that grow under the rocks. It's never more than they need; it's always just enough. It's why it's said worry is dealing with tomorrow's problems on today's pasture. There isn't enough. Live in the moment; rely on God. He supplies what we need in the moment.

he leads me beside quiet waters, (v. 2b)

I can thirst for all kinds of things, but only He knows what waters are safe for me.

In Jeremiah 2:13, the prophet wrote, "My people have committed two sins: They have forsaken me, the spring of living water, and have dug their own cisterns, broken cisterns that cannot hold water." I can be guilty of trying to take care of myself, of imagining waters other than the refreshment found in Jesus will satisfy. It's my own sin, but it leaves me vulnerable to enemy attack.

The most frequent cause of death in the wilderness is, ironically, flooding.[18] Nearby limestone mountains cannot absorb rainwater, so when the water runs into the desert, it creates sudden and violent floods that fill the *wadis* (canyons carved out by past floods). Anyone standing in a wadi when a flood comes will be swept away. The wadi then becomes dry again, but a little water from the flood will remain on the wadi floor and is attractive to thirsty flocks. A wise shepherd knows walking through a wadi can be dangerous and instead will guide his flock to quiet waters.

. he refreshes my soul.
He guides me along the right paths
for his name's sake. (v. 3)

Where do we find refreshment? In the Word. It gives me encouragement, guidance, strength, conviction. "The law of the LORD is perfect, refreshing the soul" (Ps. 19:7).

A spiritual hero of mine is Henrietta C. Mears. She was an author and became a Sunday school teacher at First Presbyterian Hollywood in 1928. Her most famous work was a book called *What the Bible Is All About*. She wasn't fancy; she simply taught and lived the Bible. Among her students were the founders of Campus Crusade for Christ, the founder of the Navigators, the founder of Young Life, a chairman of World Vision, a US president, and Billy Graham.[19] From her place in the classroom, she was a powerful kingdom advancer and understood the idea of planting spiritual tamarisk trees.

The tamarisk tree doesn't bloom for its first twenty years or fully bloom for sixty; still, Abraham, who had yet to have a child, planted one in Genesis 21:33, "Abraham planted a tamarisk tree in Beersheba, and there he called on the name of the LORD, the Eternal God."[20] Abraham, while waiting to see God's promises fulfilled, was determined to prepare for what he believed was coming. He planted those trees for his future generations' enjoyment.

I have tried to plant my own figurative tamarisk trees as a reminder and encouragement to generations ahead that God does move, but practically speaking, it's hard. It means saving when I would rather spend and speaking when it's easier to be silent. It means resolving conflict when it's simpler to pretend and investing in people when I might prefer free time. It asks of me diligence, perseverance, patience, and forbearance. None of those are my strong suits but are all critical to standing strong in spiritual battle. Henrietta Mears demonstrated a commitment to the long view when she wrote the following inside her Bible:

> I will win the personal allegiance
> of every one of my class
> to the Lord Jesus Christ;
> I will walk; I will write; I will pray.

I will remain close to them
until they are established;
I will associate with them in fellowship;
I will make myself available to them always;
I will see that they are committed to some definite task.

I will put the Cross back into my Christianity,
and I will pray as I have never prayed before
for a new vision of God.

I will spend and be spent in this battle,
and will not seek rest or ease;
I will seek fellowship with the Man of Sorrows
as He walks through this stricken world.

And I Will Not Fail.[21]

She rightly understood this is war, and God can be trusted. I like how she had declarative statements about her dreams and disciplines. I wonder how much correlation we can draw between her level of kingdom impact and this willingness to not seek rest or ease. Her faithfulness would have made her a target of Satan, but I imagine she experienced a fierce fellowship with Jesus while under attack in the darkest valley.

Even though I walk
    through the darkest valley,
I will fear no evil,
    for you are with me;
your rod and your staff,
    they comfort me. (Ps. 23:4)

When I picture a shepherd, I absolutely picture someone carrying a staff. In every shepherd painting I've ever seen, there's a staff, that crooked stick used to guide sheep back onto the path. But I love that the psalmist includes the rod, a weapon representing power, authority, and protection. I am deeply comforted my Shepherd has a rod in His hand and will use it to beat off that which threatens me.

> You prepare a table before me
>   in the presence of my enemies. (v. 5a)

If I were writing this, it would just be a table for the two of us, far away from the Enemy. But that's not what God says; He says we can sit without fear "in the presence of [our] enemies." Is that enemy satisfied watching me eat? No! He will try to pull up a chair to the table and speak to me. What does the Enemy say? "This is really bad." "Expect the worst." "You are not going to make it."

While the Devil is telling me I'm not going to make it through the valley, the Shepherd is telling me He is *with me* in the valley. I can't control who or what prowls around my table. However, as I sit there, in the presence of my enemies, I have the authority to invite to and keep away from the table anybody I want. I have power in the name of Jesus to say to the Enemy, "You do not have a seat here." He might prowl, but he can't sit down. My countenance in the presence of my enemies is my greatest testimony, and I want it to say, *I am looking at Jesus.*

> You anoint my head with oil;
>   my cup overflows. (v. 5b)

There is a Bedouin custom called the overflowing cup. If you finish whatever they have served you, usually coffee or water, they will always give you a refill. The way you signal you don't want any more is by leaving a little bit in the cup.[22] The same is true spiritually; if I keep pouring out, I signal to God I want more of Him. When I am feeling like I haven't been filled up in a while, maybe it's because I have been holding some back.

> Surely your goodness and love will follow me
>   all the days of my life,
> and I will dwell in the house of the LORD
>   forever. (v. 6)

The word "surely" shows David's unique relationship with his Shepherd. David knew as long as he was within God's plan, goodness and grace would not just follow him, but actually pursue him. I want to live like I understand my Shepherd's ability and desire to protect, pursue, and provide for me. He is sovereign over all things, especially Satan.

After studying this psalm, I have found it helpful to repeat it out loud when I sense darkness rolling in. Sometimes I simply say it at night when sleep eludes me; other times in traffic, I say it when I am feeling impatient and self-important. The other night, Todd and I were at the very beginning stages of what could have been an all-out fight, but as I softly spoke these words and promises, I found myself next to quiet waters, standing behind a Shepherd who had His rod out to defend us.

Do you think in terms of adding up the good things you've done in your life to see if you're "qualified" for heaven? If so, how can you change that line of thinking?

If I was going to make a declaration, like Henrietta Mears, what exactly would I say and could I live up to it?

When do your feelings overrule your thinking?

How has the Enemy tried to sit at your table?

Chapter 26

Hope is a rope.

"May the God of hope fill you with all joy and peace as you trust in him, so that you may overflow with hope by the power of the Holy Spirit."
Romans 15:13

When I dropped off my son at college for the first time, I wasn't prepared for all the big feelings; they snuck up on me. We had been talking about it all summer, but now it was real.

He played football, so there was a day when the parents met one another and interacted with the coaches, familiarizing themselves with the program. After we spent hours on campus, the coach said suddenly, "Okay, freshmen, huddle up. Say goodbye to your parents. I'll meet you in the locker room in ten minutes." Just like that, the moment arrived and I was not ready.

I turned to Evan and punched him in the chest. "$#%, Evan, I don't like this." His head swiveled quickly around to look at his dad. In all his years, he'd never heard me use profanity. Todd's eyes were wet with tears, and in all Evan's years, he'd never witnessed his dad cry. We fumbled our way through the next few moments, and I now know he later called his sister, saying, "College is going to be way worse than we thought. Mom is cussing and Dad is crying!"

Sometimes life sneaks up on you. You think you have all the time in the world to get ready, when *bam*! It shifts and you are not prepared.

For instance, I went on an ice-skating field trip with one of my favorite children's homes. It was pure chaos as a team of adults attempted to keep fifty small Mexican children upright and balancing on thin blades. But I

grew up ice skating, so I was loving the whole scene. Then without warning, an out-of-control skater crossed my path, and I reached for the hand
of the four-year-old next to me. The whole thing happened so fast, I don't
remember much detail of the actual impact. But there was lots of blood, a
trip to the ER, many stitches, and I have a nice scar now—and thankfully
none of the kids were hurt. Things can happen fast, and then everything
changes.

This take-your-breath-away speed of change is the idea behind Mark
4:15, "Satan comes and takes away the word that was sown in them." You
can plant the Word and expect all you need are sunshine and water to make
it grow, and then *bam*! From out of nowhere, the Enemy comes and steals it.

The Devil is against life and hope in every sense. He doesn't want us to
experience eternal life with Jesus or a life "to the full" (John 10:10) here on
earth. He is a tormentor and will bother us when we are awake and harass
us while sleep. It can feel like it's coming at you from out of nowhere. In the
middle of this war, it's all too easy for me to fixate on my own pain, battles,
and storylines and not have an awareness of where and how God might want
to use me. When I do step up and share the gospel or a truth about God's
promises to us with someone, Satan works immediately to steal it away.

Since sharing the gospel and living like God's kid exposes Satan's lies,
he combats it passionately. The gospel message is powerful (Rom. 1:16;
Heb. 4:12; Eph. 6:17) and freeing (John 8:31–32), but it requires people to
proclaim it (Rom. 10:14, 17). God set the whole system up from the very
beginning so we would partner with Him, sharing how He is working in our
lives. The Enemy will try to twist our testimonies or confuse the listeners. He
will use any tactic he can so the planted Word doesn't take root. Sometimes,
the Enemy's opposition to the gospel is overtly evil and demonic; other times
it's slippery, quiet, and subtle.

Paul was well acquainted with both forms of resistance, and he wasn't
afraid to call the Devil out. Consider this story found in Acts:

They traveled through the whole island until they came to Paphos. There they met a Jewish sorcerer and false prophet named Bar-Jesus, who was an attendant of the proconsul, Sergius Paulus. The proconsul, an intelligent man, sent for Barnabas and Saul because he wanted to hear the word of God. But Elymas the sorcerer (for that is what his name means) opposed them and tried to turn the proconsul from the faith. Then Saul, who was also called Paul, filled with the Holy Spirit, looked straight at Elymas and said, "You are a child of the devil and an enemy of everything that is right! You are full of all kinds of deceit and trickery. Will you never stop perverting the right ways of the Lord? Now the hand of the Lord is against you. You are going to be blind for a time, not even able to see the light of the sun." (13:6–11)

As we partner with God to advance His kingdom, we will meet opposers, enemies of everything that is right. As Paul demonstrated in this passage, we have to call them out so their deceit and trickery aren't successful.

The year one of my sons turned fourteen, he had an overnight birthday party with more than a dozen guests. It was all in good fun, but their basement games grew louder with each hour. Finally, after multiple warnings to settle down, I commandingly laid down the law. It was amazing how effective it ended up being. It was my house; I had the authority and I exercised it.

I used to believe being spiritually authoritative was about being loud or strong, but as I grow in my understanding of spiritual warfare, I am learning it's more about *confidence* and *hope*. Understanding what God has promised and believing the story isn't over yet give me the courage and spiritual assurance to stay in this fight. This is why I now pray every time, "With the authority I have as a co-heir with Christ …" before I make my request.

I am reminding myself and anyone listening in heaven or on earth that I understand the spiritual power that comes from being one of God's kids. It means no matter what is happening around me, I have hope.

As I grow in my understanding of spiritual warfare, I am learning it's more about confidence and hope.

The world needs hope. *I* need hope, because life can be hard and unrelenting. This is not how it's supposed to be. In English, *hope* means something abstract, like "expectation." It's hard to put your hands around expectation; it can feel like a moving target and subjective. In Hebrew, the word for *hope* is *tikvah*, meaning "cord, or rope," and the root word is "to bind; to wait for or upon." *Hope is a rope!*

We can hold on to it when the world seems out of control or when we don't know how to make it through a difficult season, like the promise given to the Israelites in captivity in a foreign land. "'For I know the plans I have for you,' declares the LORD, 'plans to prosper you and not to harm you, plans to give you hope [*tikvah*] and a future'" (Jer. 29:11).

Is it possible for a rope to give me hope? It did for Rahab. A cord of scarlet thread represented the salvation of her family. Hope is rooted in waiting, grasping (onto like a rope) the promises of God. "Wait for the LORD; be strong and let your heart take courage; yes, wait for the LORD" (Ps. 27:14 NASB).

I have a child in a hard storyline, a friend battling marriage fatigue, a sister-in-law fighting cancer … the list goes on and on. Waiting on God for relief, or breakthrough, increases my strength and gives my heart courage. I can cling to and depend on Him even when I can't see the next right step. Then I can rest, trusting the issues I'm facing are part of what God is using to transform me. The ending has already been written, so I can have hope. It's not about victory or defeat; it's more about how much collateral damage the Enemy can cause on his way to the lake of fire.

> I can rest, trusting the issues I'm facing are part of what God is using to transform me.

Jesus showed us how to fight against the failure of faith with prayer. He told Peter in Luke 22:31–32, "Simon, Simon, Satan has asked to sift all of you as wheat. But I have prayed for you, Simon, that your faith may not fail. And when you have turned back, strengthen your brothers." If we have a satanic threat against us, we can pray and ask others to do the same for us. Then we can support one another in this war that never stops.

A great cloud of witnesses surrounds us, and their testimonies remind us this life has never been about this life. It has always been about *that* one—the heavenly afterlife when we will be with Jesus. Peter tells us in 1 Peter 2:9 we are God's priests. And a priest's chief responsibility is to show others what God is like. We can't *just* be recipients of His grace and goodness; we are also to be conduits or vessels of that goodness to others. All Christ followers have a calling, and I don't mean the particulars of where we sense God asking us to be or serve. His larger mission is for us to put Him on display.

When people interact with a priest, a Christ follower, they should know more about God after the exchange. This is true whether I am delivering good news or engaging in conflict. I need to conduct myself in such a way that, on the other side of my conversations, the people with me learn more about God's character than they do about me. Maybe they understand His generosity, or His sensitivity, or His truth, or His grace, but whatever it is, it's the one task He has left us with: *represent Me through your actions to a lost world.* This is the good news we are to share.

Problems will come in the form of broken relationships, physical setbacks, and spiritual attacks, and then heaviness and grief may settle over small things as well as large losses. It can be tempting to think it will all be better when circumstances change. But the Bible tells us *there will always be another battle.* In 2 Samuel 21, we see the following storylines:

> *Once again there was a battle* between the Philistines and Israel. David went down with his men to fight against the Philistines, and he became exhausted. (v. 15)

> In the course of time, *there was another battle* with the Philistines, at Gob. (v. 18)

> *In another battle* with the Philistines at Gob, Elhanan son of Jair the Bethlehemite killed the brother of Goliath the Gittite, who had a spear with a shaft like a weaver's rod. (v. 19)

> *In still another battle*, which took place at Gath ... (v. 20)

To stand strong in my marriage, household, ministry, and life, I have to continually prepare for the daily battles. My greatest weapon is keeping the Word handy. Sometimes I use an app or play the audio Bible in the car. Sometimes it's with a journal and my heavy study Bible. Other days, I just repeat verses I earlier put to memory. The passage in Ephesians 6 referencing the many pieces of the armor of God doesn't include a sheath, because I am never to put away this sword.

Another tool I have is worship music. Listening to songs that remind me of God's truth and His promises counteracts the lies that cause discouragement and fear in me. Sometimes I listen to music really loud in my car, with the windows open and the wind on my face. Other times I put on instrumental music and let the sound comfort and envelope me. The Bible talks of God inhabiting the praises of His people, so when there is a battle, I can sing my way through it.

Praise and prayer were elements critical to King Jehoshaphat's victory over the combined armies of Moab, Ammon, and Edom in the Judean wilderness. Knowing the armies were coming, he said, "We have no power to face this vast army that is attacking us. We do not know what to do, but our eyes are on you" (2 Chron. 20:12).

Jahaziel the prophet told them not to be discouraged because of how big the army was against them: "For the battle is not yours, but God's" (v. 15). He reminded them to keep going, be obedient, stand firm, and see (v. 17). That encouragement to "see" is what I hold on to throughout my day. I can sometimes want to upgrade my gifts, or my faith, but God says it's never been about *me*: *What if you upgraded your expectations instead of* Me? *Waited and watched to "see" what* I *can do?*

The army marched toward the enemy, and "Jehoshaphat appointed men to sing to the LORD and to praise him for the splendor of his holiness as they went out at the head of the army, saying: 'Give thanks to the LORD, for his love endures forever.' As they began to sing and praise, the LORD set ambushes against the men of Ammon and Moab and Mount Seir who were invading Judah, and they were defeated" (vv. 21–22).

God used their praise as a weapon. It spoke to the hope they had in Him. They held on to their hope—like a rope—and it carried them through to victory. Paul and Silas in the Philippian jail were "praying and singing hymns to God" when the earthquake struck that set them free in Acts 16:25–26. In all the moments when I feel overwhelmed, I play praise music and trust God hears my heart's cry to agree with His truth and fight, when I can't.

I am challenging myself to take walks with friends, to speak up when I hear someone feeling hopeless, to make the calls I am prompted to, and to tell my stories while listening to others. We were made for connection. This is the glory of later telling war stories together—for God's glory. Whether I whisper my prayers, write them, shout them, share them with others, say them in the morning—whenever and however I connect with God, talking to Him provides what I need to get through "this" new battle. When I engage in biblical practices, I see God deliver what I need: mercy, patience, self-control, love, peace, joy ... In the end, the result of that fruit in my life makes me grateful, instead of bitter, for the battles I face.

Who told you the gospel, and how was that work opposed?

What are you holding on to right now with hope?

What battle are you facing now, and what are the spiritual implications? What can you do now?

Conclusion

Sozo

"I will redeem you with an outstretched arm."
Exodus 6:6

Todd and I met in March of 1990 when I was a high school junior. I remember teasing him that he was a month late because I had spent February 14 watching other girls receive flowers and chocolate, wondering if that would ever happen for me. The next day, I was called out of first bell for a delivery of roses he had sent to my high school, along with a witty note wishing me a happy Valentine's Day. Then every period for the next seven, another bouquet of flowers arrived, until I went home after school with both my arms and my heart full. This is what a man in pursuit looks like—over the top, all out on the table, you can't miss it.

As romantic as Todd was and still is, he's just a reflection of my heavenly Bridegroom. God is infinitely more feeling, demonstrative, and sacrificial. His pursuit of us is unrelenting. Take for example His language toward us as His bride. He chooses us, pursues us, and stays even when we are unfaithful. In both the days of Moses and the time of Jesus, God used culturally familiar language to communicate how much He loves us. But first we have to understand how men pursued women in ancient times.

A man in ancient Israel would tell his family he was interested in marrying a woman, and they would ask him to write down the history of their relationship and also the histories of the two families. The document would have covenantal promises he would make to the woman (for example, he wouldn't love anyone else). It would be too long to fully copy, so he would make two summary documents—one for each family.

Then the man and his family would come to the bride's household, and he would offer her a cup of wine as a symbol of proposal. By drinking it, she was saying yes. As a sign of their engagement, he would hand her a gift. Throughout the ages, it was a coin; today, it's a ring. This gift was promissory and meant he was coming back. He would share one of the two copies of the summary document that included details regarding: the right of the greater party to make the covenant, the obligations of each party, the penalties and benefits of the relationship, and the history of the relationship. It detailed promises, such as respect me, don't want another husband, and don't mistreat me and I won't mistreat you.

At this point, the man would go home to prepare the bridal chamber, and only when the groom's father said it was ready would it be considered finished. This usually took a year, and after the father's approval, the groom's family would go toward the bride's home, announcing their arrival with trumpets or a shofar.

The bride's family had been waiting throughout the year and would indicate their readiness with lit torches or oil lamps. Together, the bride and groom would move under the canopy, called a "chuppah." It symbolized no one was in this relationship other than the two: not an ex-girlfriend, mother-in-law, or friend. One of the many ways Satan destroys marriages today is by pushing more people under the chuppah than just the bride and the groom.

I share this background because now I want you to imagine the scene through the Ten Commandments, since it follows the stages of an engagement. (God's people would have recognized it as a wedding!) God shared with us our history with Him in the Torah, the first five books of the Old Testament. Through Moses, God gave many covenantal promises for His people during their courtship:

I will take you out.

I will set you free from slavery.

I will redeem you.

I will take you as My people.

Continuing with the wedding imagery, "On the morning of the third day there was thunder and lightning, with a thick cloud over the mountain" (Ex. 19:16). The thunder was like trumpets announcing the groom, and the lightning like the torches the family carried to get to the bride. God as the Groom went and prepared a place for them, the Promised Land. The cloud came over, like the chuppah, and covered the mountain. He gave us His summary document, which we call the Ten Commandments. In fact, Moses carried down two identical stone tablets, arguably two summary documents, further proven by one copy going into the Ark of the Covenant (Ex. 25).

One commandment reads, "Remember the Sabbath day by keeping it holy" (Ex. 20:8). Sabbath is our date night! Imagine how confusing it is to our Groom when we neglect this time set aside for Him. I was in Israel over Sabbath once and enjoying a day at the beach. An Israeli man started a conversation by asking if I was American, and could I answer a question for him? I winced, not knowing what was next, but I nodded. "Is it true in America, you don't observe the Sabbath? Why *wouldn't* you want a day when you could rest, reset, restore yourself, and connect with family and God?"

I smiled with regret. "Not only do I not observe the Sabbath well, I end up doing extra work on that day to catch up or get ahead." The Sabbath should demonstrate our commitment to a relationship with God. What am I saying when I am busy on that day, even if it's doing His work?

In the first commandment, the first word is *Anochi*, which means "I" in the Egyptian language ("*I* am the LORD your God").[23] Why would God start the very first of the Ten Commandments in a foreign language and not in Hebrew? At that time, the Jewish people had just come out of Egypt. Although they used the Hebrew language, Egyptian was common to them. God chose to communicate in a familiar language, creating mutual ground with which to start off the relationship. What breaks my heart is at the wedding in Sinai, God's bride wasn't delighting in her Groom, but making a golden calf. He knew His bride would be adulterous, and He picked her anyway. Just like He knows I will be unfaithful, and He picks me anyway.

Then came Jesus and the New Covenant. He included all the elements of a groom in pursuit, showing us in every way He wants us. He offers up the cup to us today, just like the groom offered the bride. With it, He's saying, "Come into covenant relationship with Me; I pick you. Get under the chuppah with Me. Don't let anyone else come between us."

As for the coins, now through the Holy Spirit, He gives us many gifts. James 1:17 says, "Every good and perfect gift is from above." Sometimes I offer the gifts He gave me to another. Other times I pretend my gifts were of my own doing. And He gave them to me still, knowing it would be so!

One day, trumpets will announce the arrival of our Groom. "For the Lord himself will come down from heaven, with a loud command, with the voice of the archangel and with the trumpet call of God, and the dead in Christ will rise first" (1 Thess. 4:16).

He urges us as His bride to be watching and waiting with our lights on, indicating our readiness. "Be dressed ready for service and keep your lamps burning" (Luke 12:35). "Don't hide your light under a bowl" (11:33).

He has left us since the proposal and is preparing a place for us. This Promised Land is a space to be with Him forever, and we'll know it's ready when the Father says so. "And if I go and prepare a place for you, I will come back and take you to be with me that you also may be where I am" (John 14:3).

When I took the cup, I said yes to Jesus. Yes, I want in that relationship. Yes, I believe He is coming for me one day. Yes, I will be faithful. Yes. This relationship is a journey of saying YESYESYES!

Our enemy can't force me to do anything (Acts 26:18), but he can scare me into saying no. He's hoping I say no more than yes. He wants me to doubt the proposal and to lose hope God is coming back. All that disbelief will cause me to step out of line or to sit down and look around for another groom. It might cause me to be a busybody or falsely believe I need to earn His love. Satan's tactics are one giant distraction plan. If he can interfere with God's relationship with me, he can make headway in this war. If I stay connected to my Groom, I am safe and protected.

I see it reflected in my relationship with my earthly groom. When I tell Todd no, when I am too busy to spend time with him, or when I place other priorities above him, our relationship struggles. We have to fight our way back to each other, and because we are both sinful and selfish, it's hard. But God is perfect, always there, always committed, always faithful, always ready to receive me. There's no groveling or proving myself. He wants me just as I am.

There's no groveling or proving myself. He wants me just as I am.

The Greek word *sozo*, which is translated "saved" or "salvation" in the Bible, actually means three things together: "save, heal, and deliver." It's not just a onetime saving, when we went from darkness to light. It's His response over and over again when we call on Him. It doesn't matter how relentlessly the Enemy attacks us, or how badly our sin has messed things up, God will never stop coming to our rescue.

As He is putting us back together, or touching places where we need healing, He will use all things together for our good, transforming either our circumstances or us in the midst of those circumstances. I use *sozo* as an English word, calling on Him to bring His heavenly angel armies to battle on my behalf.

Sozo. Come for me; I feel overwhelmed.

Sozo. Heal me; I am broken.

Sozo. Deliver me; I am tempted.

Sozo. Save me; I am lost.

This is the chorus we sing to our Groom, who never tires of answering.

I was at a conference in college, and the speaker told a story of a Rwandan man in the 1980s who had been converted to Christianity through a missionary. His tribe was opposed to his new faith and threatened him with death if he didn't renounce God. Given one last chance, he was told the next day would be his last unless he refused Christ. He stood strong and was martyred. Found among his belongings was a journal in which he wrote the night before he died.

This was the first time I heard his final writings, and I recall standing up spontaneously in the middle of its reading. I wanted my body language to reflect the *yes* I heard in my heart. Since then, I've reread it on days when I feel battle weary and need reminding that even when I am weak, in Christ I am strong. I want to give this spiritual brother of mine the last word in this war book of strategies. While reading his commitment and willingness to die for our faith, may we be inspired this day to fight without relenting.

I'm part of the fellowship of the unashamed. I have the Holy Spirit's power. The die has been cast. I have stepped over the line. The decision has been made—I'm a disciple of his. I won't look back, let up, slow down, back away, or be still.

My past is redeemed, my present makes sense, my future is secure. I'm finished and done with low living, sight walking, smooth knees, colorless dreams, tamed visions, worldly talking, cheap giving, and dwarfed goals.

I no longer need preeminence, prosperity, position, promotions, plaudits, or popularity. I don't have to be right, first, tops, recognized, praised, regarded, or rewarded. I now live by faith, lean in his presence, walk by patience, am uplifted by prayer, and I labor with power.

My face is set, my gait is fast, my goal is heaven, my road is narrow, my way rough, my companions few, my Guide reliable, my mission clear. I cannot be bought, compromised, detoured, lured away, turned back, deluded, or delayed. I will not flinch in the face of sacrifices, hesitate in the presence of the enemy, pander at the pool of popularity, or meander in the maze of mediocrity.

I won't give up, shut up, let up, until I have stayed up, stored up, prayed up, paid up, preached up for the cause of Christ. I am a disciple of Jesus. I must go till he comes, give till I drop, preach till all know, and work till he stops me. And, when he comes for his own, he will have no problem recognizing me ... my banner will be clear for "I am not ashamed of the Gospel, because it is the power of God for the salvation of everyone who believes ..." (Romans 1:16)[24]

Sozo. Amen.

What's Next?

Reading this book represents quite an investment of time. I pray it will save you from the unwanted and unintended consequences of spiritual inactivity. We are all invited into a spiritually aggressive posture, and it starts with understanding the authority we've been given in Christ. Kingdom advancement is at stake, so thank you for learning along with me what it means to throw the first punch.

As a way of ensuring an awareness of and engagement with the spiritual becoming a natural rhythm in my life, I created the acronym COMBAT. Each letter represents a step in this spiritual fight: *C* is for confession, *O* is for observing the tactic the Enemy is employing, *M* is for measuring his impact, *B* is for believing what's true, *A* is for aiming our weapon, and *T* is for throwing the first punch. In the past, I might have unwittingly helped the Enemy, but walking through these letters in recent years when I become aware of a battle has stopped me many times from contributing to an enemy agenda instead of experiencing victory in Christ.

This book's companion guide, *Punch First*, was born from the desire to have material to activate us in our own battles and also have something to exchange with trusted friends. COMBAT is what I work through when I am feeling a pressing temptation or a chaotic situation. In each day of the 21-day guide, there are exercises designed to challenge and enlighten us, questions for journaling or discussion, and Bible verses for further understanding and personal illustrations.

Here is an excerpt from day 1 to give you an idea of how it works. In the end, it's what we *do* with our understanding (not just what we know) that will make the difference in our lives.

DAY 1

How This Works
A Tale of Two Storylines

I was on a walk with my husband, Todd, and we were planning a getaway for just the two of us. Although the conversation started with the right intention, before long we were irritated with each other, disagreeing on where to go, how much to spend, how long to be away … We walked for a while in silence until Todd had the wisdom to ask, **"What do you think the Enemy wants to happen here?"**

Although in that moment I still wanted to win the argument, and I didn't want to go anywhere with Todd, I knew he was asking the right question. Underneath all my big feelings and selfish thinking, the truth is I would rather work *with* Todd *against* an enemy who didn't want us to connect, or rest, or dream than work *against* Todd *for* the Enemy.

We can partner with God to see regrowth and rebuilding, or our sin nature can partner with the Enemy, and without wanting it, we can propel forward the goals of the Devil. Paul wrote, "Put on the full armor of God, so that you can take your stand against the devil's schemes. For our struggle is not against flesh and blood, but against the rulers, against the authorities, against the powers of this dark world and against the spiritual forces of evil in the heavenly realms" (Eph. 6:11–12).

In 1 Peter, we read about an enemy roaring around like a lion, wanting to devour us. I believe the lion is circling, and I want to take a stand. I am tired of the teaching that says to put on the armor and wait for the Devil to come to you. **What if we decided to go after *him* and punch him first?**

✵ Write out 1 John 3:8 here:

God has invited His people to partner with Him ever since Genesis. Sometimes that is building a kingdom of heaven here on earth, and sometimes it's collaborating with God to destroy the Devil's work. I don't have to sit around and be frustrated about the state of the world, or the struggle I have with a particular sin. I am biblically encouraged to dismantle what the Devil is constructing around me. Since all work by God—restoration, reconciliation, redemption, rescue, and repair—is opposed by our spiritual enemy, I can imagine with stunning accuracy the Devil's agenda.

Instead of restoration, he wants destruction. Instead of reconciliation, he wants us to remain in conflict. Instead of redemption, he wants us to experience shame; instead of rescue, he wants us lost; and instead of repair, he wants us to feel permanently broken.

The Enemy will tell stories through our lives. When we don't put up a fight, and instead hand our sin nature over to him, he'll use it against us. There is much that factors into how we think, feel, and act—our past experiences, generational sin, spiritual discipline, temperament, accountability … We can learn to see beyond what is unfolding around us and train for the spiritual combat we are invited to engage in.

When I was finishing as an interim lead pastor in a church, it was time to introduce the staff to my permanent replacement. I started a chapel with this question, "If you were the Enemy, what would you do over the next month to derail this ministry?"

The team immediately responded:

"Cast doubt over the new pastor's intentions."
"Create misunderstanding in meetings or over email."
"Divide us over something seemingly small."
"Craft competition or jealousy."

I shared, "When you see any of these potential situations unfold, rightfully assign blame to the Enemy, who is biting on our insecurity or unconfessed sin (or someone else's). Let's confess any of our own wrong thinking and ask a blessing over whomever else is in the story."

This was more than a situation where humans decided if their personalities would mix well with others. It was a spiritual battle with the Enemy's goal of keeping God's people critical of one another and distracted. We brainstormed ways to play spiritual offense, including initiating with the new leader and praying for his adjustment. We imagined a culture with short accounts, where everyone gave the benefit of the doubt and sin had no soil to flourish. The result was a community of hopeful sojourners, not perfect, but in motion, proactive, and healthy.

Let's start this journey by thinking through the contrasting storylines we see at work in the world today. **In the chart below, list God's storyline along with its enemy counterpart.**

GOD'S STORYLINE	ENEMY'S STORYLINE
Peace	Chaos
Gentleness	
Hope	
Sacrifice	Selfishness
	Fear
Reconciliation	
	Destruction
Grace	Condemnation
Love	Hate

I now walk into every situation asking myself these questions, *What would the Enemy want to happen here? What's his agenda?* so when

I see (for example) fear, harshness, selfishness, or chaos unfold, I know to fight against Satan and not the people in the story. Punching first is owning a distinct strategy where I invite peace into fearful conversations, or purposing to be graceful when I sense harshness, or disciplining myself toward generosity when I'd rather be selfish. We don't react when attacked, but instead move the spiritual momentum in the direction of kingdom advancement.

Todd and I are walking alongside a couple who is struggling in their marriage. Our own punch-first strategy is to make sure we are investing in each other, knowing if we aren't strong, we will be less likely to believe we have something to offer them. We have a child graduating from high school this year without a clear plan, and our punch-first strategy is to remind him of what we do know, so while the Father of Lies whispers to him, he has something to hold on to.

When I see every story and conversation as spiritual, I feel commissioned to spiritually fight. It's different from waking up and acting a certain way because of how I feel. I don't have to wonder if he wants to attack my self-image, family, marriage, friendships, and ministry. I know the Devil wants me spun around and confused. He wants me silent and ashamed. I don't want to wait for his attack while on defense. I want to offensively take ground from him. He does the same things over and over again; we can read about his tricks in Scripture and testify to his tactics in our own lives. We don't need to tiptoe around the Devil or hide from him. Knowing he's coming, we can learn to spot him from a mile away. How do we protect ourselves and those we love?

❧ Everything is spiritual, so what's a situation you are facing right now, and what do you imagine the Enemy really wants? How could you make a spiritually offensive move?

❧ Paraphrase Luke 10:19 below. What does it tell us about our spiritual power?

❧ What questions do you have about evil or enemy activity?

John 10:10 promises that God wants us to have a life "to the full." It's worth fighting for. The world God created is good, but it's not always safe. Some of the not-perfect-and-unsafe experiences are a result of living in a fallen world. We get sick, people die, and it's not fair. Some of the not-perfect-and-unsafe is because we sin or others sin, and the consequences are destruction, conflict, loss, and brokenness. Finally, some of the hard we experience is designed by our adversary, who is relentlessly on the attack.

Could we know this to be true and live a life where we advance spiritually, rather than just, at best, hold him back? What if we became so adept at offensive sword wielding that God would ask us to fight for others?

About a quarter of everything Jesus talked about in Scripture had to do with spiritual warfare. He knows how much it impacts our lives and is pleased when we willingly engage with Him in battle. The most powerful spiritual step I can take is to walk into every room and ask, *What would the Enemy want to happen here? What's his agenda?*

> *God, teach me to have eyes to see that what's happening around me is spiritual. I want to come to You with my questions and to be led by You. Show me the spiritual power You designed for me to wield in Your name. I am Your child and student. Amen.*

Notes

1. Bill Petro, "History of Telemachus: the Monk Who Ended the Roman Gladiatorial Games—January 1, AD 404," BillPetro.com, January 1, 2021, https://billpetro.com /history-of-telemachus; and John Huffman, "Telemachus: One Man Empties the Roman Coliseum," Discerning History, September 15, 2016, http://discerninghistory .com/2016/09/telemachus-one-man-empties-the-roman-coliseum/.

2. Study: *Gospel Transformation*, Serge Ministries. Show: *Real Life with Beth and Rob*, Family Talk radio.

3. This story taken from *Start with Amen* by Beth Guckenberger. Copyright © 2017 by Beth Guckenberger. Used by permission of Thomas Nelson. www.thomasnelson.com.

4. C. S. Lewis, *Mere Christianity* (New York: McMillan, 1952), 164–65.

5. The trauma training came from Trauma Free World, https://traumafreeworld.org/.

6. For more on *go'el*, see Ray Vander Laan, That the World May Know series, www.thattheworldmayknow.com/.

7. Curt Thompson, *The Soul of Shame: Retelling the Stories We Believe about Ourselves* (Downers Grove, IL: IVP Books, 2015), 93.

8. N. T. Wright and Michael F. Bird, *The New Testament You Never Knew: Exploring the Context, Purpose, and Meaning of the Story of God*, video (Grand Rapids, MI: Zondervan, 2019).

9. For more on *mamzer*, see "What Is a Mamzer?," My Jewish Learning, accessed July 7, 2021, www.myjewishlearning.com/article/the-mamzer-problem/; and Jay F. Guin, "Faith Lessons by Ray Vander Laan: An Unlikely Disciple," One in Jesus, October 21, 2009, https://oneinjesus.info/2009/10/faith-lessons-by-ray-vander-laan-an-unlikely-disciple/.

10. Graham Cooke (@GrahamCookeBBH), "You can tell the quality of someone's inner life by the amount of opposition it takes to discourage them," Twitter, February 26, 2015, 11:10 a.m., https://twitter.com/GrahamCookeBBH/status/570979191388278784.

11. Thompson, *Soul of Shame*, 22.

12. For more on listening to heal the brain, see Bessel A. van der Kolk, *The Body Keeps Score: Brain, Mind, and Body in the Healing of Trauma* (New York: Penguin, 2014).

13. Story originally told in chapter 12, "José Angel," of my book *Reckless Faith: Let Go and Be Led* (Grand Rapids, MI: Zondervan, 2008).

14. "Mahalia Jackson Prompts Martin Luther King, Jr. to Improvise 'I Have a Dream' Speech," History.com, accessed July 7, 2021, www.history.com/this-day-in-history /mahalia-jackson-the-queen-of-gospel-puts-her-stamp-on-the-march-on-washington.

15. "'I Have a Dream' Speech, in Its Entirety," NPR, January 18, 2010, www.npr.org/2010 /01/18/122701268/i-have-a-dream-speech-in-its-entirety.

16. Thanks to Pastor Chad Hovind for the Romans 14 study prompt.

17. Gervase Vernon, "Dr. Janusz Korczak: Hero of the Warsaw Ghetto and Educator," *British Journal of General Practice*, October 2018, www.ncbi.nlm.nih.gov/pmc/articles /PMC6145982/.

18. Oishimaya Sen Nag, "Did You Know That More People Drown in Deserts Than Die from Dehydration?," WorldAtlas, March 13, 2019, www.worldatlas.com/articles/did-you -know-that-more-people-drown-in-deserts-than-die-from-dehydration.html.

19. Judy Douglass, "The Amazing Legacy of Henrietta Mears," *Starting Fires in Minds and Hearts* (blog), March 8, 2013, https://judydouglass.com/blog/2013/03/the-amazing -legacy-of-henrietta-mears; "Woman of Vision," Gospel Light, accessed July 7, 2021, www.gospellight.com/henrietta-mears/; Matt Brown, "The Hundred Year Influence of Henrietta Mears," *Outreach Magazine*, August 9, 2018, https://outreachmagazine.com /features/evangelism/32507-hundred-year-influence-henrietta-mears.html; and "Henrietta Mears," Wikipedia, accessed July 7, 2021, https://en.wikipedia.org/wiki/Henrietta_Mears.

20. Carolyn Adams Roth, "Abraham's Symbol of Commitment," *Delving Deeper* (blog), May 15, 2019, www.carolynrothministry.com/post/abraham-s-symbol-of-commitment; and Chris Schultz, "The Tamarisk Tree," *The Well* (blog), October 5, 2015, https://thewellcommunity.org/blogs/the-well/the-tamarisk-tree.

21. Henrietta Mears, quoted in David Guzik, "The Decision of Henrietta Mears," Enduring Word, July 7, 2019, https://enduringword.com/decision-henrietta-mears/.

22. I learned of the Bedouin customs from my own experiences. See also David Patterson, "The Overflowing Cup," *For Family and Friends* (blog), October 25, 2013, http://family-friends-others.blogspot.com/2013/10/the-overflowing-cup.html; and Eugene Peterson, *Psalms: Prayers of the Heart* (Downers Grove, IL: InterVarsity Press, 2000), 59.

23. Menachem Schneerson, "Shavuos: The Egyptian Word 'Anochi,'" Chabad.org, accessed July 7, 2021, www.chabad.org/therebbe/article_cdo/aid/2300790/jewish/Shavuos-The -Egyptian-Word-Anochi.htm.

24. "The Fellowship of the Unashamed," Maranatha Bible Church, accessed July 7, 2021, www.mbcmi.org/wp-content/uploads/2015/10/The-Fellowship-of-the-Unashamed.pdf.

Bible Credits

Unless otherwise noted, all Scripture quotations are taken from the Holy Bible, New International Version®, NIV®. Copyright © 1973, 2011 by Biblica, Inc.™ Used by permission of Zondervan. All rights reserved worldwide. www.zondervan.com. The "NIV" and "New International Version" are trademarks registered in the United States Patent and Trademark Office by Biblica, Inc.™

Scripture quotations marked ASV are taken from the American Standard Version. (Public Domain.)

Scripture quotations marked CSB are taken from the Christian Standard Bible®, Copyright © 2017 by Holman Bible Publishers. Used by permission. Christian Standard Bible® and CSB® are federally registered trademarks of Holman Bible Publishers.

Scripture quotations marked ESV are taken from the ESV® Bible (The Holy Bible, English Standard Version®), copyright © 2001 by Crossway, a publishing ministry of Good News Publishers. Used by permission. All rights reserved.

Scripture quotations marked KJV are taken from the King James Version of the Bible. (Public Domain.)

WANT TO CONTINUE THE FIGHT?